Doing Business in Japan

Doing Business in Japan

A Peek into Cultural Forces
Defining Corporate Japan

Mark Smith

The author can be reached at:
marksmithjapan@gmail.com
Website: us-japan-gps.com

Dedication

To Toshio Asano, PhD

A brilliant scientist, businessman, and former President of Asahi Kasei Corporation who taught me so much about Japan and Japanese business. Without his mentoring and care, my career in a such a traditional and competitive Japanese corporate environment would have come to a quick and disastrous end.

Acknowledgements

My time in Japan was extensive and I interacted with so many people from all different walks of life each of whom has contributed in one way or another to this work. There are too many to name and a comprehensive list may well be longer than the book. I offer special thanks to Barbara Corrigan; Asano-*san;* John Costantino; Tamada-*sensei*; Oe-*san;* a close friend and his wife who declined to be named; Saito-*san,* Sasahara-*san,* , Sakamoto-*san,* Sanae-*chan,* Takada-*san,* Michael Stever, Nagai-*kun,* Kinuyo, Nori-*chan*; Hiroyuki Hayashi and his ever-helpful wife, Mariko; everyone at Fuji Aikikai and Numazu Aikikai; everyone who ever floated in and out of the band; and all the good people who helped with the annual Fuji Festival.

Contents

Introduction

First and foremost, I want to emphasize that this work is not a criticism of Japan, the Japanese people or the Japanese culture. There are very few absolutes in the world. Socially relevant behavior is, for the most part, forged by a people's culture. Among other things, it is predominantly a mixture of history and religion.

As the world shrinks through improved communications and transportation, and as the nuclear age and the fall of the Soviet Union have brought a more equitable balance of power across the globe, people are ceasing their black and white analyses of each other. In fact, the majority of western countries have now become accustom to dealing in only shades of grey. As so many useless but costly wars have shown us in the past, there is no standard way to do things; many paths can lead to the same place. Our challenge in this 21st century is to lose our fear of the different and to learn how to improve our own station without denigrating someone else's.

Our exposure to these "different" ways has increased in

the past two decades. Businesses, in particular, are constantly challenged with reconciling their concepts and values with those of foreign partners. In the last 20 years, new markets have opened up and, along with them, the potential for new opportunities. One of the major problems with transitioning from a company's present market base into these new frontiers has been how to interact on a cultural level. "Business as usual" is a phrase we can relegate to a long-lost era. There is no "usual" when you are trying to understand the motivations and desires of a market that has been closed for over 50 years. Yet and for some reason, the old players expect that these new players will close this gap overnight and that the western business fairy will sprinkle them with magic dust and they will wake up in the morning with a complete understanding of how "our" business models work.

But as anyone who has been engaged in international business well knows, this just isn't possible. At best, the formation of a cross-cultural partnership comes through a long, arduous process involving countless hours of preparation, study, and interaction. At worse, business enterprises are formed through a bulldozer effect with the two parties slogging through numerous problems, and only with a great deal of luck can they arrive at an agreeable conclusion. But no matter if you take the proverbial high road or the low road, it all takes a significant amount of time.

And time is one asset that we value too highly to have treated like penny stock. As Americans, it is part of our heritage to always be looking for ways to be more efficient; that is, to obtain the same result but using less in the way of available resources. Especially time. For managers and corporate leaders, this search is a never-ending process. After all, this is an advantage that can put an individual or a corporation heads and shoulders above the competition.

In no other arena has this become a more unachievable task than when trying to conduct business in Japan. Japan has one of the largest economies in the world—an attractive motivator to western companies. It is both a large consumer and a large manufacturer. This translates into something for everybody. But dealing with the Japanese can be a tiresome, confusing, and frustrating experience. While America has a great deal in common with other western countries, it has almost nothing in common with Japan. It truly personifies the definition of "different."

The Japanese economy is strong and stable, rivaling many of its western counterparts. While a shadow of its hard charging bullish days of the 80s, it still occupies an important and influential position on the world stage. The large corporations have been steadily resuming foreign acquisitions though on a much saner scale than in the past. To date they seem to be avoiding their former flamboyant purchases where the goal was, historically, to hold the "record" for the amount of money spent, and, in the end, lost. Many of the players of that age have long since retired from business, but there is enough intuitional memory to where the mention of those days of yore makes them a bit uncomfortable in their failure to retain such dominance.

One marked difference between the "bubble" Japan enjoyed in the 80's and the situation that exists today is that the world has grown smaller and more connected. Additionally, the western players are in a better financial and political position than before and are, consequently, better possessed in the way of bargaining power. I think that there can be little doubt that anyone—at least at this juncture—entertains any thoughts that Japan Inc. can reclaim their eminence of days gone by. The playing field is simply too level and the players are too many.

But only a fool ignores the lessons of the past. Since it may be unavoidable to do business on some level with Japanese companies in the future, it may be a good idea to prepare oneself to enter that fray. If no other tools are mastered, at the very least one must be armed with enough arrows in the proverbial quiver to survive the experience with one's sanity intact, which, in itself, is no small feat. For while "business" as perceived by the rest of the world has evolved, for some reason the practices found in Japan are still largely reminiscent of samurai swords and kimonos.

It is often difficult for westerners to live among the Japanese and not develop a sense of frustration. Part and partial to this is that the cultures are at polar opposites. If an American feels an instinctive urge to go right, his Japanese counterpart will inevitably have an equally instinctive urge to go left. It may be that an analysis of history, culture—past and present—and social structure can shed light on why this is so, but, in the end, the "why" doesn't so much matter as the "what" and the "how." What is the effect, and how does one either (i) change that; or (ii) use that to an advantage. Sadly, there are no blanket algorithms to apply; each situation resembles a work of art, a one of a kind Van Gogh. By concentrating on "process" and on reasonable expectations, we can hope to control the business dealings to a greater extent and better predict and shape their outcomes.

Keep in mind that there are very few large Japanese companies. For a country with a population of 126 million—about half that of the US—this at first comes of somewhat of a surprise. Japan—despite it being only the size of California—has efficiently organized its industrial machines into large businesses supported by an array of small- to medium-sized business. These latter elements surround the main production centers of the large companies and prosper by obtaining outsourcing contracts. Traditionally, this symbiotic relationship was seen to be the responsibility of the heavy industry, which, more often than not, supported an entire city with its related business. In fact, some of the more recognizable Japanese companies—Toyota, Hamamatsu, Kawasaki—are actually named by the cities from which they originate.

In a day and age that is rendering manufacturing functions to the cheap labor of the third world and shifting focus on developing "soft" products, *e.g.*, information technologies, Japan is now finding it harder and harder to maintain its manufacturing edge. China has assumed the mantel of the world provider of cheaply manufactured goods. Korea has all but displaced Japan in the production of quality electronics and is making a push to dethrone Japan in the automotive industry. For the Japanese, its traditional development and labor costs are taking bigger and bigger bites out of profits in the present competitive environment.

5

This has resulted in a shift in philosophy; particularly, towards a large corporation's obligation to keep smaller "mom and pop" businesses liquid. The large heavies are feeling less and less of a social obligation to keep these shops operating. Instead, they are focusing their main efforts on trying to maintain their own internal lifetime employment structure. Outsourcing still plays a large role in any corporation's operations, but now competition has made it into more of a buyer's market rather than a seller's one.

Western companies generally deal with this problem by building critical mass, usually through a run of mergers. In Japan, however, this is like two lepers arm wrestling, and—if I may borrow a line from Robin Williams—every time two things come together, they quickly fall apart. The reasons for this are legion, but are mostly due to trying to conduct a merger in the true sense of the word: Two equals coming together. Each company struggles to keep its own corporate identity throughout the merger process while, at the same time, trying to wrest control of the sacred personnel department. This tends to be a formula that often proves more of a problem than first imagined, and one that inevitably leads to a parting of ways. In short, M&A activity inside Japan—that is, a Japanese company with a Japanese company—has not historically met with a great deal of success. One exception seems to be with some of the larger, more global pharmaceutical companies. They have awakened to the epiphany that their futures lie outside the confines of Japan, and have taken steps to achieve the size and product lines they need to become and remain competitive worldwide.

This leaves few options for the small- to mid-sized companies looking for ways to survive. Globalization has also rained on their parade in that their survival almost always involves an encounter with a foreign (non-Japanese) business. In some ways, the need for Japanese companies to interact outside their borders has been both a boon and a bane for western companies. Japanese companies are eager to partner with a western company if for no other reason than to establish itself internationally. However, they remain as enigmatic as ever, and understanding the process and the "rules" by which they play the business game is not so easy. Only through persistence and in trying to capitalize on the opportunities that lie with this small archipelago have western companies managed to experience the level of success to date.

These experiences have left a wide array of impressions. Some companies find the experience a mild inconvenience but worth the trouble considering the returns. Others find it downright nerve racking and endure the process only with the promise of access to a new market or a new product line. Very, very few walk away after working with Japanese and feel it was "business as usual." Frustrations arise at several different levels and what westerners assume is a worldwide industry practice they soon discover is an unheard concept in Japan. There is a lot of "re-inventing the wheel" that goes on and this takes up a whole bunch of time that companies do not factor into the process. Additionally, you find yourself frequently dealing with situations that you, in your wildest dreams, could never have imagined. Again, this takes up a considerable amount of time to sort through. Throughout the deal making process you will catch yourself wondering which will occur first: the conclusion of the deal; or you going insane.

In all fairness, it is difficult to point the finger solely at the Japanese. After all, the reason westerners deal with them is because they have something they want. The problem is: Are you willing to endure the pain to achieve your goals? By properly preparing for the encounter, doing a little bit of research, and developing a strategy that can alleviate much of the posturing that takes place, you can both shorten the amount of time needed to conclude your business, and you can avoid the heartburn and frustration of hitting a brick wall at every turn. Concisely put, the best advice was given over 3000 years ago by, ironically, a Chinese philosopher named Sun-Tzu who wrote, *"Know your enemy as yourself and you will never know defeat."*

There have been a number of people who have looked at Japan Inc. from the outside and have generously offered their opinions and observations. Some have even proven helpful. But there is only so much one can glean from this vantage point since secrecy is inherent to the Japanese system. Everything that westerners see is one type of façade or another and is likely what the Japanese want them to see. Access into the inner sanctum of corporate Japan is not granted to *"gaijin."* But don't feel too badly, not all Japanese are not allowed in this elite clubhouse either. Nevertheless, the information to which you want access lies within this inner circle, and if you had a source that could penetrate that and relay to you what goes on there, you could, ideally, anticipate what unexpected hurdles will appear in front of you and how to overcome or—better yet—skirt them. The process would flow much more smoothly and, in the end, the relationship between you and your Japanese partner would be less strained, perhaps even amicable.

And this is where I lived for past fifteen years, working in the licensing department of a mid-sized pharmaceutical company. During that time, I have experienced first-hand several business deals and negotiations with both US and European companies. I have been invited to behind-closed-doors strategy meetings and have seen the criteria used for proposals and counterproposals. Every step of the way I was constantly challenged to put things into some kind of perspective from my western born and raised sensibilities. On occasion, and when permitted, I was able to use my position as the "native speaker" to voice my thoughts on the situation at hand and how best it should be handled. Over the course of several years and a number of lost battles, I came to understand how to successfully get ideas across in light of what priorities ruled the day.

There are no guarantees in business. Every deal, no matter where and with whom, is a gamble. All you can hope to do is minimize the risk, and play the cards dealt you as best you can. When beginning any dealings with a Japanese firm, it is first prudent to understand in what context the Japanese operate on a day-to-day basis so that it becomes easier to reconcile the way in which they actual do business. In this respect, the preparations needed are no different than when entering the fray with any other company in the world except that there is very little in the way of common ground.

No doubt, other Americans have experienced the inner workings of Japanese companies more and on a much grander scale. I'm sure that their opinions would also be very useful—I know I'd like to hear what they have to say. But in this work, I've attempted to keep things simple. The last thing any corporate negotiator wants to do is spend countless hours in an in-depth study of the Japanese culture, language, and business acumen. He has other, better things to do. The advice contained here is by way of an introduction and overview—there is a much finer degree of subtlety that is best acquired through long experience or by proxy of one who has had the experience for you. Please do not leave with the impression that this work imbues some form of mastery over the subject. If it were so easy, there would scarcely be any need for it. By sticking to basics and leaving the finer details up to business development types who have immensely more experience in deal making, I would like to reduce the analysis to a few simple guidelines while, hopefully, shedding some light on the enigma we know as Japan.

History and the Social Hierarchy

Before one can tackle the task of dealing with the Japanese, it is important to know in what context they conduct business. What things are important to them? What are sensitive areas? What kind of thinking processes do they employ? All these things stem out of who they are and how they've developed as a people. Once understood and held up to the values and ideals that are firmly rooted in the western psyche, the process of conducting business can be a much easier undertaking. As a bonus, particular strengths and weakness can be played upon adding to the overall value your company can gain from the experience.

But Japan is a complex society with a plethora of contradictions—at least from a western perspective. Why do people who have developed anti-bacterial plastics and porcelains engage in eating raw food laden with all kinds of live microbes? Why are you required to take off your shoes before entering a house only to find the dwelling ripe with layer upon layer of dust and mildew? How can a society who provides some of the best electronic devices in the world be so computer illiterate? To get at the core of these anomalies we need to go back in time and take a look at the progress of the nation from its inception.

Japan is one of two countries in the world that can boast a single, uninterrupted chain of rulers from the same imperial family for over 1500 years. Denmark would be the other. It became a civilized, albeit warlike, culture somewhere around 660 B.C. and developed a certain, unique, and advanced technology compared to its peers at the time. When the European states were neck deep in anarchy and barbarism following the fall of the Roman Empire, the Japanese people were mastering several different art forms ranging from sword making to glazed pottery [or "japanning," the term for which the country Nihon (or Nippon) has been called by westerners].

And this really is the essence of the people: Whatever they do, they do to perfection. This limits their individual experience to only one or two major areas, but whatever expertise is pursued, it remains their focus for life. There is not a great deal of cross-training in Japan. In this way they have master the division of labor. If everyone does his or her part, every aspect of life is provided. And this works well for them. It has been only relatively recently that they have strayed from this tried-and-true algorithm. Modern companies try to shift people around internally from position to position to round out corporate skills. The problem is that Japan Inc. is still exploring how to do this with any degree of efficiency and focus, so instead of getting a balanced middle-aged employee being a jack-of-all trades, what you get is an employee that believes he has mastered several components of the business world. In reality, he has a Cliff Notes exposure to these aspects of business and, in the end, is ill-equipped to function at a competitive level in any of those components.

Without delving too deeply, it is practical to mention some important aspects that were prevalent during the roughly 375 years of military rule during the shogunate (*Edo jidai*) that preceded the modern era when the emperor was restored (*Meiji jidai*) and technology growth began. First was the presence of a caste system. Mainly there were three divisions among the people. In order from top to bottom, those castes were: Samurai; Agrarians; and Merchants. All these supported the nobility in a feudal system very similar to that found in early European history. One distinct difference was their extreme— fanatical by our standards—devotion to duty and to their caste. This extended to the point of death. There was little hesitation in sacrificing one's life for your liege lord (*daimyo*). This was especially true of the samurai class whose duty it was, often enough, to do exactly that. In return, the feudal lord provided protection for those residing in his fiefdom and provided the samurai with lifetime employment.

Throughout this entire period, it was the policy of the ruling military board to prohibit interaction with foreigners of any sort. To do so was punishable by swift and certain execution. As a result, the doors to Japan were sealed for almost 400 years. No great loss to the west, but it had dire consequences for the Japanese. While technology was advancing at a breakneck pace in the rest of the world, the Japan culture remained frozen in time. The arrival of Admiral Perry's black ships spewing smoke and laden with cannon served as a wake-up call. The spirit of the Japanese was willing but being relegated to what amounted to be, comparatively, the Stone Age, they could not interact with foreigners as equals. Westerners, even then, were undiscerning with regard to the Japanese. Relying only on their five senses, they perceived an undeveloped and crude civilization not so dissimilar to what they were finding throughout the Pacific. And so these colonialists treated the Japanese with the same disdain. Then, as now, the Japanese show you what they want you to see, not what really is. The result was several countries fiercely competing for trade agreements and contracts. No matter which country prevailed in this bidding war, Japan was the ultimate winner.

Commodore Perry's armada served as an abrupt awakening and was the impetus the aristocracy needed to shake off the chains of the military dictatorship. As with many things Japanese, the system may change faces and names, but the underlying psyche remains the same. In this case, they exchanged one dictator for another: Shogun for the Emperor. And so, a new era was ushered in. Exit the Edo Era; enter the Meiji Era. But the system had changed in name only. Gone were the samurai. The feudal system was banished and the samurai were suddenly without jobs. Laws prevented them from carrying their swords—something which had, for so long, set them apart from the ordinary and served as their elite status symbol. The noblemen quickly adapted and used what remained of their wealth and influence to establish ventures and businesses that exploited the westerners' imperialistic appetites. This was our first taste of frustration, one that that would continue to grow until peaking in the mid-1980s.

Eventually, modern day corporations would fill the vacancies left by the feudal fiefdoms. They would employ samurais of a different nature: The Japanese "*salaryman.*" The underlying principles of the corporation and the "*kiretsu*" were exactly the same as under the 1,400-year-old feudal system. Under its "*new*" iteration, the salaryman would devote his entire life to the company. Everything—family, friends, self-fulfillment—played a distant second. In return, the company would provide for his every need, the most important of which was a lifetime employment system.

Consensus is everything; individuality is nothing.

This could be the mission statement for Japan Inc. There is and always has been a great focus on the group rather than the individual. This stems partially from their great division of labor. The individual cannot survive. Everyone must be assimilated and enter the continuum. Mavericks do not fare well in Japan and seeing a successful Japanese entrepreneur is as rare as a four-leaf clover. Times are changing in this respect, though at a snail's pace. The bursting of the bubble really emphasized how badly things could get when everyone is wrong.

You will find that Japanese businessmen shun decision-making without first developing a consensus internally.

Nothing in Japan has substantially changed, at least from a social structure point of view, since the first

Japanese emperor, Jimmu, reigned in 660 B.C. It is always a wonder how such a country can keep so steady and constant a social system in the light of such a volatile and rapidly changing world. Even major disruptions like World War II did not provide the spark for a cultural revolution. Some superficial reforms were made but mostly at the insistence of the occupying forces. The underlying system did not; Japan continues to employ the same basic social and, by extension, business templates.

Nationalism

An integral part of the Japanese psyche is a strong sense of nationalism. The Japanese are a proud people. They always have been. Don't let all the humble bowing and head bobbing fool you. One only has to look at their attendance at the Olympics or World Cup Soccer games to get a rough idea to what extent they express their nationalism. This nationalism extends regionally as well. Attending a baseball game anywhere in Japan is a far cry from watching the Mets at Shea Stadium. Try getting a ticket to a Nagoya Dragons or Yomuri Giants game on game day. Sold out. Anyone who remembers going to Shea as a kid in the early 1970s, would never stop to think that reserved seating would be required for a baseball game.

There are few places in the world where nationalism is so overtly vented against anyone who is not "of the blood." For centuries, the Japanese have maintained their racial purity. One historical reason has been that access to the country was denied to all but a very few, so there were no marital options for the Japanese man or woman except

17

with their own kind. Unlike the states in Europe whose borders changed with regularity, being an island further helped isolate Japan. Another underlying reason was that during feudal Japan, it was virtually impossible to marry outside your caste. For that matter, it was unlikely that you would marry outside your village. All these factors contributed to the single Japanese people that still very much exist to this day.

As more and more foreigners began their influx into Japan, the Japanese government, whether by design or reflex, has consistently put insurmountable barriers in the way of integrating them fully into society. In a way, this keeps all the undesirables out, but is akin to throwing the baby out with the bathwater. It is virtually impossible to be naturalized, and even after setting up residency, it is extremely difficult—bordering on impossible—to obtain the vote. The Japanese naturalization process is designed specifically to dissuade people from becoming Japanese. There are six criteria one must meet to become naturalized: (i) residency in Japan for five consecutive years; (ii) be over 20 years old and "responsible" under Japanese law (in Japan 20 years old is the age of emancipation); (iii) be financially able to support yourself and your family; (iv) be without other citizenship or being willing to renounce any former citizenship; and (v) be of "good behavior." The Justice Ministry shrouds this whole process in secrecy and, as a rule, never discloses why a request for naturalization was denied. They have been known to ask applicants or their neighbors questions ranging to what food the person eats to seeking out compromising intimate details about the applicant's sex life.

The Justice Ministry has also been known to ask you to change your name so that is sounds more Japanese. This is no joke. The goal is not necessarily to find you acceptable, but to find something that would label you as *un*acceptable. But the proof is in the data pudding. In 1999, 16,120 people were naturalized in Japan compared with 839,944 for the same period in the US. In 2000, the number dropped in Japan to 15,812 while it rose to 888,788 for the US. In 2015, the number dropped even further to 9,469 while the number in the US was 730,259. For a country with about twice the population of Japan, the US lets in about 55 to 77 times more people join its citizenry than Japan.

As foreigners have slowly penetrated the workplace, Japanese firms have responded by establishing one set of rules for the Japanese workers and another set for the foreign staff. One is fully endowed with the corporate benefits while the other is given benefits piecemeal. These rules are not only endorsed by the company, but the central government as well. Pensions and health plans are doled out niggardly or not at all. Mandatory contributions made to retirement accounts or to the government welfare system have not been, until recently, reimbursable beyond five years to a foreign worker and then only when he or she returns to his or her own country. Everything under these systems seems to prod the foreign worker to abandon his or her post and to return home.

Within the minority residents, some races have preferential treatment over others. The people who surprisingly are subject to the most scrutiny are those who arrive in Japan from other parts of Asia. Caucasians do experience this separation to some extent, but Koreans, Chinese and Philippinos lie at the very center of it. The prevailing attitude at immigration offices is that Caucasians will abide by the laws of Japan and do little to disturb the peace while peoples from Asian countries will disabuse the system; that is, not pay taxes, exploit the national health insurance, become involved with under the table—or underworld—activities, and the like. But perhaps the most underlying motivation is that, eventually, the majority of the Caucasians end up going back home. They do not present themselves as a burden to the Japanese socialist system.

All these protectionist measures come from a certain phobia that the majority will eventually become a minority in their own land. It boils down to control. If they can control the foreign element, then they can eliminate any potential threats to its social system brought on by these elements. One way to do this is to give the government carte blanche when dealing with non-natives. Strangely enough, it bears a remarkable resemblance to the way the Romans dealt with non-citizens during *Pax Romanus*.

If possible, steer clear of national issues that may be occurring on the Japanese front at the time of your meeting and, above all, do not be baited. Often times Japanese will ask your opinion about a certain tidbit of news that affects both the US and Japan or that is the subject of world attention at that moment in time. More than likely they are just testing their English out on you and, since the majority of Japanese have little diverse political awareness, they may not be all that cognizant of what they are asking. Certainly, they haven't prepared themselves for what they are about to hear. They have seen a lot of television and harbor a preconception that Americans are all politicians to some extent. In an attempt to make small talk, they choose a particular "hot" topic more or less at random. And as Americans, we love to talk. And talk, and talk. It is our fatal flaw. In your reply to whatever is queried, fight this genetic predisposition and say as little as possible in the most neutral—but polite—way you can.

Women's Role in Modern Japan

Almost everyone has heard stories of the traditional Asian woman. They can be summarized with a single word: Subservient. Historically in Japan, the fate of women has been no different than that of their Asian sisters. Traditionally, women were more like possessions to be used rather than people to be reckoned with.

As children—and again I'm talking ancient history up through the early 1950s—women were relegated to household work. Very few thought that educating women would amount to anything. It was just a waste of time. When they reached marrying age, that being somewhere between 16 and 19, the parents made arrangements either through direct negotiations with relatives or friends, or through a marriage broker to secure husbands for their daughters. A woman's single mission in life after this point was to produce a male heir. In feudal Japan, to ensure their dynasty persevered aristocratic men made use of concubines. Later as the military feudal system was

22

displaced by a type of business feudalism, marriages were used more and more by the common people to connect families and thus increase or consolidate power bases on a number of levels. In this respect, an early-mid-20th century woman's plight increased only marginally from her 17yj century forebearers.

This is not to say that all women have always been completely powerless in Japan. There have been several examples throughout their long history where the women were the puppet masters, holding power over deferential husbands. But this is far the exception and not the rule. In general, they were the instruments that maintained a man's home and, as such, were completely at his beck and call.

There is one aspect of the man-woman relationship that never fails to strike us Americans as particularly odd, especially considering how deferential woman have been cast. Japanese men customarily delegate to their wives the responsibility for all the family finances. A man rarely concerns himself about household money. One reason may be that money was traditionally considered a petty and dirty item. We need only look at the social status of merchants who traditionally held the lowest caste in the feudal system. As a rule, men never touched money except as it related to political expediencies.

And this is still true for much of the population today. But don't confuse being responsible for finances with being able to dispense with the finances as you see fit. With whatever salaries their husbands bring home, they must provide for an impossible number of things. First, is the basics: Food, clothing, and shelter. In a country where a 324 square foot apartment in Tokyo can cost more than

$1000 a month, and where eight slices of bread cost almost $1.50, this can be very challenging. Add on top of that the money that needs to be saved for your children's schooling (Japan does not have a free educational system beyond middle school nor does it provide for loans to help pay for university expenses), the cost of the supplemental night schools for your teenagers (*jukus*), various additions to the bare bones health care system, and the staggering costs of transportation, and you've entered into the budgeting balance nightmare of a housewife.

On top of trying to juggle all of this comes the stress of working in the wants and desires of the man. Generally, a man will get a monthly "allowance" (*o-kozukai*) from his wife which can range from ¥15,000 yen to ¥40,000 yen (very roughly $150 to $400) depending on how old he is and how much money he brings home. This allowance is meant to cover petty expenses like coffee, cigarettes, the occasional night out, newspapers, magazines, club dues and the like. Special events, such as company hail-and-farewell parties, club events, or group outings are extra line items that the wife needs to be prepared to budget, and usually at a moment's notice as these may or may not come with advanced warning depending on the disposition of the husband. Sudden urges to buy computers, gadgets, or other boys' toys can come at any time and the wife is expected to provide them out of hand. Naturally, the expense of the item may play a part and the item may turn out to be unattainable. As a rule, the wife traditionally needs to be creative in her money management and be able to perform some voodoo economics.

24

For the most part, wives do not work at full-time jobs; they do not work at all while the children are in elementary school. Her job is to stay home and, basically, raise the children. The man's single focus is his job. But as difficult as a man's job may appear to be, to follow a housewife through a typical day is to know what the word "grueling" means. It looks something like this.

The wife needs to be up before the rest of the family in order to prepare lunches (*bento*) for the children. This is not as simple a task as you may think. It's not your mom slapping two slices of bread around some peanut butter and jelly, throwing it into a brown bag with a handful of Doritos and an apple and calling it lunch. A Japanese schoolchild's lunch box is more along the lines of a work of art. They are elegantly laid out with a wide variety of treats. School children often compare lunches and there is a sense of competition on whose has the best presentation. Some mothers go even so far as to cutting cartoon characters or other such designs into thin slices of cheese or ham. The ubiquitous serving of rice almost always is garnished with a happy face or some such design. All this takes an inordinate amount of time to cook and prepare.

Once the lunches are finished, it's on to making breakfast. Typical breakfasts consist of grilled fish, rice, and soy-based soup (*miso*). Again, think of the time it takes. Only then can she wake up everyone and begin shuttling everyone off to work and school.

During the day, there is the daily shopping to be done. Japanese live in a culture where "fresh" takes on a wholly different meaning as it is measured in hours and not days. Many families still shop one day at a time. The expiration dates on food are considerably shorter than what we are used in America. And aptly so, as much of the food is eaten raw; *e.g.*, eggs, fish, and some meats. Food tends to be consumed within two days with leftover being the basis for lunches. This means that a housewife needs to visit the market roughly everyday. Just think of your experience dealing with the trip to the supermarket: Parking, traffic, and waiting in lines—lines which are long in Japan since nearly *everyone* shops for food *everyday*. Now take this experience and imagine living it every single day for the rest of your life. Once they get home from their shopping they clean, do laundry, and air out the bedding (*futons*).

It can be a rare experience where the entire family eats at one sitting. This bodes ill for the housewife who may need to prepare dinner up to three different times over the course of the evening: Once for the smaller children, once for the junior/senior high school students who come home later due to their extracurricular activities or night school (*juku*), and again when the husband comes home, usually late in the evening. Then, of course there's the usual clean up: doing the dishes, wrapping up the leftovers, and taking an inventory to identify what needs to be bought at the market the next day. While immersed in these activities, she may be called upon to deliver adult libations to her husband during his "relaxation time," generally in front of the television.

This first to rise last to bed routine goes on until the youngest of the children has entered junior high school. Then the housewife is free to get a part-time job. This is on top of everything else she has to do. Virtually all the money earned goes towards the children's education or to the household savings.

Not that it's a lot of money. Housewives, still being responsible for the daily operations on the home front, can only take part-time jobs that fill the empty hours when the children are not home. This relegates them to service jobs or menial labor jobs. In short, mindless work with no real prospects for a solid future. Some wives even take "in-home" jobs. These are jobs for which they are paid piecemeal; *e.g.*, stuffing envelopes, preparing circulars, arranging promotional items.

Then there is the "in-law" effect. A goodly portion of Japanese men live with their parents, even after marrying. This is especially true of the elder sons (*chounan*) as they stand to inherit the family estate, such as it is. It is a dark, dark day for the new wife to have to move into the man's home with his parents. Despite any olive branches she may carry or however attentive she may be to husband and the children, as long as the mother-in-law lives, she is doomed to a life of merciless persecution. The mother-in-law dotes on the son/husband and feels that no other female can provide for him in the fashion that he deserves nor in the manner he is accustom *viz.* as she has always provided for him. As a result, the new wife gets blamed for every little frown or sigh that escapes the man, regardless of its cause. Few men stand-up for their wives in these situations, and their only advice is, "Please cooperate."

But why do women tolerate this lifestyle? In part, it is due to who controls the system. Looking at the opportunities available to women can go a long way in understanding their situation. Many women now attend college. Some do quite well, and, overall, I tend to believe they are on par with their American counterparts academically. They are well represented in several disciplines and graduate competitively among their male peers. That's about where equality, as we understand it, ends.

Employers do not like to hire women into positions that have career tracks. Because an overwhelming number of women do not work after having children—some, in fact stop work after marriage—they are considered a bad investment. No employer wants to go through all the trouble *vis-à-vis* time and expense to train a woman and add to her professional development only to have her quit after five or six years of working.

Yet large corporations always ensure to hire plenty of young women to do the menial office work. These "OL's" (*office ladies*) are rarely ever hired for their prowess at dictation, or computer savvy, or organizational skills. They are hired, more often than not, to provide (i) eye candy for the men in the company; and (ii) potential wives for the younger hires.

Now, as with anything, there are exceptions to the rule and these exceptions are growing albeit at a slow pace. You will find Japanese women occupying management positions with companies. None ever rise to the fill the CEO's shoes, but some do manage to become "managers," (*kachou*) and even "general managers" (*buchou*) at least in the Japanese sense of the word. They can have careers of sorts, but there is no hope—and they harbor none—of entering the elite strata of blue-chip corporate executives. Inevitably they all dead-end in their pursuits whether it is in their mid- to late twenties via marriage or in their forties when they max out on the corporate ladder.

The man's view of all this has been virtually unchanged since the feudal era. Women in general are no less the objects they were 200 years ago. Many are paraded nude in weekly magazines or daily newspapers. Businessmen can commonly be seen reading these publications commuting to and from work. This practice purveys the entire nation and it is passed down from one generation to another. Women are even represented in Japanese comic books (*manga*) as sex objects and with generally disproportionate features. Both adult and teenage men publicly indulge in this literature.

During your business dealings with Japanese companies, women will inevitably play different roles. You can easily identify what niche they occupy and what place they will hold in the business deal you are undertaking. If they appear in uniforms—a practice still very, very common for female office workers—and you tend to see them only during breaks, they are basically the servants. They may act as ushers bringing you to and from the meeting room from the reception areas. Always wearing very pleasant smiles on their faces which are sometimes accompanied by muted giggles, they bring coffee or tea, and make sure lunch is delivered on time. They'll be there after your team leaves to clean up the conference room or to prepare for your continuation meeting the next day. They are generally very shy and will avert their eyes if you can per chance make eye contact.

Being Americans, you'll have a tendency to want to be chivalrous and "help." Don't. Be polite, thank them…you can even hold the door for them, but don't trespass on their duties. They are not supposed to be noticed, and if you choose to dote on them, you attract attention to yourself in the process. The Japanese will undoubtedly sarcastically comment on your "American-ness" (*Sasu ga America-jin da ne*...or something to that effect). Outwardly they will be amused but on the inwardly they may wonder what kind of a person pays attention to something that is supposed to be considered invisible. It could be construed as a kind of weakness.

If woman in business attire attends the meeting, her role can be varied. Since many women in Japan are better at English than men, she may be taking notes on what transpires. If this is the case, she will generally be the last seated and usually it's in the corner somewhere. There are times when a woman will apparently chair the meeting. Don't be misled here. Depending on her age, she may be a protégé and her manager chose your meeting to see how she is progressing. Even if she has a great deal of experience in hosting meetings, she may just be a showcase. Her role here is one of an emcee and not as lead negotiator. Look for the senior person near the center of the table opposite you.

In situations like this there are two roads you can take. One is to be patient and let her run the meeting as she translates to her colleagues and defers to them on every point/inquiry you make. This does burn up daylight and can be a bit taxing on the nerves. But it is progress. Be aware, though, that your dialog is through her and not at her.

In any meeting, to zero in on the senior member of the group, watch the Japanese team when they are engaged in internal cross talk. It happens a lot so don't be alarmed that something is awry. The key person will undoubtedly be the gentleman who talks least and in the most unanimated, dark, and soft voice. Almost without fail, the members who are discussing the issue at hand are making a pretense of talking with one another while they are, in actuality, directing their dialogue to this Quiet Man. When he speaks, a few seconds of silence follow. This is out of respect.

The second way to deal with this is to try to circumvent the emcee and focus directly on the decision maker. This doesn't always work and is not a recommended path. The Japanese tend to be a bit threatened when someone is so very overtly direct, but the more compelling reason not to try this approach is to give the Japanese an "out" if the discussions seem to be stalled or seem to be tanking. Going through proxies allows the senior person to quietly realize the downturn in negotiations and allows him to step in and "save the day."

No matter how you approach a business situation involving a Japanese woman, refrain from commenting on the use of Japanese woman in business or comparing it to what their roles are in the west. It may offend your sensibilities, but it is their culture and you are not going to change 1500 years of culture in day, a week, or a month. Keep focused on the goal: Getting the deal done.

Educational System

When I first came to Japan, an expatriate living there told me that if I wanted to know how something works in Japan, think about how the same thing works in the States, and then it would be the exact opposite. This advice works in no better situation than when trying to decipher how the education system in Japan functions.

Like America, Japan has nursery schools, kindergartens, elementary schools, junior high schools, high schools, trade schools, and universities. Like America, public schools are free while private schools are costly. But while the US guarantees a full 12 years of free education for its youths, Japan only provides schooling for its children through middle school. Even so, nearly all students do attend high school. This means that unless the child can get into a public school, the parents need to plan on paying tuition that can range from $100 per month to over $800 a month, depending on the school. Entrance exams are required for the majority of high schools and the competition is fierce among public high schools and those high schools that act as doors to the good universities.

It's not only upon entering high schools that entrance examinations are used, but a great number of other schools at any level—both public and private—can employ this as an enrolment criterion as well. This can begin at specialized nursery schools and kindergartens. Parents approach the examination process with deadly seriousness and spend no small amount of time learning what is being tested and then training their progeny accordingly. Thus, the emphasis on test taking begins early and spans the entire course of the child's education. With this function taking top priority, there is little or no recognition whatsoever of creativity. Conformity is the grease that turns the academic wheels. The pressure on children to succeed on these tests is enormous, and contributes greatly to the unusually high rate of teen suicides in Japan.

An example that may emphasize this focus on conformity is where, in mathematics, they learn a single method to solve a particular problem. Westerners solve problems using an array of techniques understanding that there is more than one way to reach the same solution—especially when it comes to mathematics. But in a Japanese setting, should you use algebra to solve a word problem instead of the proscribed method taught by the teacher, the answer is, unbelievably, wrong regardless of your ability to prove that your answer is correct.

Brilliance in Japan is more correlated to memory than critical thinking.

So, children from the time they can remember, are virtually programmed to this thinking process; a process that stresses repetition, conformity, and that requires some sort of precedence in order to be valid. In other words, little in the way of creative thought. Even in their approach to research, they tend to use methods that have been firmly established by other people before them. Many of the proprietary technologies in a Japanese company can be traced back to the combination or re-combination of a number of previously established technologies.

Japan has "career tracks" in education. The kindergarten that a child is able to enter in some ways determines what elementary schools for which he can apply. The elementary school, in turn, paves the way for a selection of junior high schools and so on and so on. Some schools are designed so that once you enter, you are guaranteed slots in its, or its affiliate's schools. A number of reputable universities are fed in this manner. It eliminates, to some degree, having to go through the selection process *vis-à-vis* the need to test and interview students at every inflection point. It also ensures that the individuals entering these types of universities are armed—both academically and dogmatically—with the attributes that the school values most and for which the school is likely nationally reputed.

Perhaps the single most difficult examination any student takes is their entrance examinations for college. Like the US, which uses the nationally recognized standardized American College Test (ACT) or the ubiquitous Scholastic Aptitude Test (SAT), the score of the Japanese national test, the Central Test (*senta shiken*), is used to determine which universities you are eligible to

34

apply. In the course of applying to these universities, however, you may also need to take that university's entrance exam. Those who make the cutoff are then interviewed. Those that present themselves well at the interview are offered seats in the next freshman class.

Since test taking is the primary skill that is needed for passing these exams, students often attend special schools at night geared to hone these skills. These preparatory schools (*juku*) are, in themselves, highly competitive in their bid to enroll as many students as they can. They are also very, very expensive adding to the burden of a family's finances. On the average, they run between $400 and $600 a month, which is on top of whatever school tuition you already pay for your child to attend high school.

High school students who fail to pass any of the college entrance exams need to wait a year before trying again. During this period, they are referred to as "renegades" (*ronin*). Since the backbone of the Japanese education is rote memorization—the most volatile of brain functions—these ronin need to attend schools during the year to keep the edge on. It will be a good 10 months before they are eligible to take the college entrance exams again. As with the night schools for high school students, these schools are not cheap. An appropriate preparatory school needs to be chosen depending on the level of the university a student is trying to enter. As one would expect, there is a direct relationship between the prestige of the university sought and the cost of the prep school.

As in America, there are several different strata of

universities in Japan. The tier that carries the most power in the job world is the one that contains the national universities. These are the hardest to be accepted at but the ones that land you the best jobs. Any graduate from Tokyo University (*Tokyo Daigaku*) need not worry about finding a job. He or she simply says. "Tokyo University" at job interviews and like Ali Baba's "Open Sesame" doors are flung open and red carpets laid down. Todai, as you may hear it referred, loosely resemble Harvard in distinction, prestige, and academic quality. Like Harvard, the alumni network is vast and strong, and, like Harvard, the name itself invariably guarantees employment. Most CEOs in Japan—particularly when talking about big companies—attended Todai. On the heels of the national institutions is a thin layer of private universities that include Keio and Waseda. While not considered on par with Todai, these institutions are highly esteemed and are a virtual guarantee of a job.

All the other universities in the country competitively fight for the scraps leftover by the heavy hitters. Few Japanese high school graduates want to attend any of these schools, but due to the standards and quotas of the national and the elite private universities, they are left with little choice.

With the economic situation being as austere as it is, major companies are aiming at a soft landing for its employees while still trying to maintain their lifelong employment systems. Many large businesses have put hiring freezes into effect while offering early retirement to workers 55 and over. Those who have been taking on new hires have been doing so at a trickle pace and there are often not enough jobs to offer the graduates of the top tier universities. Consequently, high school kids are under even more pressure to get into top schools in hopes for a job in their field of study. Oftentimes, settling for an initial job that is something less may mean being shut out of their professional altogether.

Attending an average university has farther-reaching effects than just difficulties in getting a job. In the grand scheme of things in Japan, this ultimately defines who you are and who can become. It governs one's life as surely as the caste system in India. Your career track is predestined despite what innate abilities you may have or what you may learn as you progress through post-academic life. In short, your boundaries, both economically and socially are predetermined by the time you are 18 years old.

One interesting note: Graduating high school in Japan is as difficult as graduating college in the US; graduating college in Japan is as difficult as graduating high school in the US. Your *bona fides* in Japan are made upon entering the university, not on exiting one. Once you matriculate, the curriculum is remarkably easy, comparatively. The system assumes that if you were smart enough to get in, you deserve a diploma AFTER putting in the prerequisite time.

To attain a university degree is often a matter of marking time. I am now speaking in generalities, there are some very brilliant graduates coming out of the system. The majority of Bachelor, Master, and PhD graduates, however, are mass-produced and might as well have rolled off the assembly line at Toyota. When looking at post-graduate education in particular, when we see a continuous educational track from Bachelor's to PhD, it is signal that something is wrong. What it tells someone reading that resume is that the person couldn't get a job out of college, and, incredulously, is likely inferior to peers that were immediately employable. It is not uncommon for Japanese companies to pay for their employees to go back to school for their post graduate studies. Moreover, in some technical fields—like healthcare—a person can earn their PhD by publishing a number of papers on their research.

Criteria for post graduate degrees vary. Some are as stringent as we would expect while others are unbelievably lax. Case in point: I had the opportunity to assist a biochemistry PhD candidate with her thesis. Although not possessing a doctorate myself, I am familiar with the process in the US and know that your thesis and its subsequent oral defense are the crux of the whole program. It needs to be something novel, something nobody else has done. It needs to be something that can be published. The observations that I made upon reading this particular individual's thesis were quite distressing. The thesis itself barely spanned ten type-written pages. It covered a subject matter that was already well documented making the chances for publication very, very slim. In short it was just an elaborate experiment confirming what some other clinician had already proven. No novelty, no in-depth analysis, and no new data.

I asked a number of scientists working in my company if this work was on par with other PhD level submissions. Much to my surprise, I was assured that it was. I was further surprised to hear that this was recommended by the student's professor. This suggested something else quite distressing: Do the university professors get some kind of validation by having graduate students verify and comment on their work, and is that the basis for granting doctorates?

When names are being tossed around to fill positions, or when a particular person is being discussed, inevitably one of the first things out of someone's mouth will be "He went to such-and-such university." This will set the stage for ensuing discussions and be pivotal in the final decision. It is amazing to see men in their late 40s and early 50s communicate with one another. Deference is almost always given to the person from the best university. And even at that age, a person's accomplishments matter less than his university affiliation.

Ability or ambition can get you only so far in Japan. Far preferred to these qualities are conformity and reputation. By reputation, I mean a perception conferred on you from the company you keep rather than from your own personal track record. Again, it is the concept of the group rather than of the individual. If you appear to belong to a certain group, then it can be reasonably assumed that you possess the identical characteristics for which the group is recognized. It would never cross anyone's mind, not even for a fleeting moment, that you are in any way, shape, or form, even a little bit different from your "group." Thus, the achievements of a graduate from Tokyo University, are seldom taken into consideration when deciding if he should sit on the board of a blue chip Japanese company.

In your interactions with the Japanese, it is likely that

someone will mention to you that so-and-so-*san* went to Todai, or Waseda, or Keio or some other top tier school. You are meant to understand what that means and the remark is to impress. It is a contextual accomplishment and regardless of your thoughts on this and in lieu of genuine appreciation, it generally pays to feign respect.

The Corporate World

After leaving the hallowed halls of higher education, it's time to enter corporate Japan. The interviewing process is very similar to the US and Europe but a bit more controlled by the professors. Companies recruit once a year. They send out recruiting parties—if they are hiring—to the various institutions from which it has typically and historically drawn. Note that each company has a list of it own pet universities from which it likes to recruit. There are rarely any professional recruiters at this point. Instead, alumni from the company go back to see what talent is available and carry their recommendations back to the personal department.

The alumni sent to the university by the company generally begin by contacting their old professors. These professors in return offer a list of names they recommend for hiring. This, generally, is a very short list and you can be sure that no matter how many students are eventually interviewed, these elite will make the final cut forwarded to the company's personnel department.

There is little to be said for the dress of the interviewee; they all are cloned to wear the ubiquitous navy blue with white shirt and regimental time. About the only things that that the younger generation does to stand out against their elders is to: (i) have three buttons down his coat and not the two that ordinarily reflects business conservatism; (ii) use huge knots for their ties; and (iii) have long, floppy shoes. This "fashion" dies once the graduate has been with the company for a year or two.

Candidates from this "good old boy system" are then pared down to the company's hiring quota for that year. The members of this short-list are called in for another interview, but this time with a representative of the personnel department. This is the person that needs to be impressed. Interview topics will range from a candidate's hobbies to of what a typical weekend consists. There is almost an intentional lack of discourse on the job being sought or the technical qualifications needed by the interviewee. The reasons are many but can be summarized by saying that the interviewees qualifications were satisfied upon his entrance into the university. The fact that he graduated verified this. The chief characteristic that the company is looking for now is the candidate's ability to blend in with the corporate culture. The company figures that it can—and will—teach the graduate anything he needs to learn on the job, EXCEPT the predominant social skills that are needed to meld with those already on the rolls of the company. To be hired, the candidate will need to, at some point in the interview, swear fealty to the company and commit to it as their first choice.

By US standards the interviews run a bit long. As

Americans, we feel that if we could remain engaged in a job interview for 30 to 45 minutes, we did well. In Japan, a so-so interview can easily run an hour or more. If the two sides really click, it can be longer. Time is not a good indicator of impact or interest.

If there is a fit, offers are made and accepted. Like the interview process for universities, there is no "shotgun" approach to job-hunting in Japan. The candidate is looking at a decision that will affect the rest of his life. The company at which he ends up accepting an entry-level position is almost without fail the company from which he will retire. Consequently, a job seeker focuses his efforts on only a handful of select companies. If he is following the advice of his university professor, he stands a good chance at getting a job.

Year after year, a list of the companies that are most popular with college grads is published. But perception is everything in this regard. As with their western counterparts, there is a kind of "dreaminess" to the expectations of the Japanese job hunter. The eyes are big envisioning the whirring of technical gadgets and the inventing of gizmos. Before the first interview, many find themselves drafting their acceptance speeches for the Nobel Prize in (fill in the blank). But what you see is not always what you get. In Japan, companies do not always recruit to fill specific positions, but for a number of foreseen vacancies. For example, a graduate student in biochemistry may be attracted to a pharmaceutical company in the top ten. He may interview and be one of the lucky few that gets an offer, but in the end, he really doesn't know what he's signed on to do. Not everyone will become a research scientist. In fact, only an elite few will get that pleasure. The others will be distributed as the personnel department sees fit and where there are technical openings. It not uncommon for a pharmaceutical company to hire more than its quota of scientists and then select what it needs in the way of researchers from that field. The remainder goes on to be salesmen or to fill other peripheral jobs.

Every company has its own individual indoctrination program. Since they hire only once a year, all the new employees will get indoctrinated together. During this process, the company will filter out who goes where internally. Once an employee gets situated, his on-the-job training begins. In the US we are expected to hit the ground running after 90 days; that is, to be performing in an unsupervised, competent manner. In Japan, a biochemist with a PhD can be expected to wash out test tubes for about a year, among other sordid and sundry tasks. For the next few years after that, the most technical jobs to which he will need to apply himself are still mindless activities. During this period, an employee is "earning" the trust and confidence of his superiors and of his peers while simultaneously demonstrating his dedication to the company. There is more of an integration focus rather than a core competency focus. The thinking behind this is team building, and cooperation goes farther than unleashed *mensa*. Everyone needs to know their place and not color outside the lines. This means that no thinking outside the box is allowed; especially, for the younger—and presumably less clever—employees.

As careers progress, one relation becomes evident to foreign observers. Older equates to wiser. The attitude of managers is that they themselves are, by nature, at least 10% smarter than the people they manage. This attitude permeates deep into the corporate structure. It is virtually unheard of where—absent a huge disparity in university—a younger team member appears to be smarter or harbor better, more efficient ideas than his elders.

Along the same lines, promotions are given on the same basis: age. Most companies purport to have a pyramid system whereby not everyone is promoted to the next level thereby thinning the number until the taper reaches the president or CEO. While true to some extent, it is not quite linear. It is largely a socialist approach as it takes into account the average lifestyle of its workers and where that worker should be in the grand scheme of typical Japan life. It is quite a challenge to find a businessman in his 40's that has not attained some sort of a managerial level position. Once a salaryman enters his 50s, a culling takes place and only a very select few will continue on an upward career path. Again, this culling will favor less ability than Todai graduates.

For entry-level compensation packages, here, at least, university affiliation has no bearing. All new employees get pretty much the same deal. These are barebones salaries based on the often very accurate presumption that new employees tend to either live with their parents at home or in company "dormitories." While called "dormitories," they are a bit cruder than what springs to mind and rather than a campus-type building, the actual building resembles an army barracks replete with a small mess hall.

The employee gets his first lift at marrying age, around 27. Similar promotions correspond almost perfectly to a family's increasing budget: Birth of children, purchase of a home, and children entering a wide range of schools that require tuition; *e.g.,* high schools, preparatory schools and universities. An average worker will reach his salary apex when he hits between 50 and 55 years of age. Depending on the financial state of the company, some employees may receive reductions in pay or "invitations" to retire early.

Companies justify pay decreases on the basis that the employee no longer needs such a large compensation package. His children should be finished with or on their last legs of higher education and his house should be paid off. This just leaves him and his wife—just as when the employee first started with the company, thus completing the work cycle. There is, however, an income source to offset a pay cut: The housewife should have a part-time job. This inflection point stresses the importance of being inside the box at all times. For employees who have strayed from the ubiquitous Japanese life paradigm, the divergence may result in hardship.

Again, it is interesting to note that the wages and benefits in Japan are fairly consistent among employees of the same rank. Occasionally, a company will offer incentives whereby a good evaluation by your manager can net you some additional cash. But by and large this extra money doesn't amount to much and is rarely worth all the backbreaking work one needs to do to obtain it. This fits well with their underground socialist ideals: No one co-worker is better or worse than his other co-workers.

This is intended to encourage harmony and productivity in the workplace.

The mandatory retirement age in Japan is 60 years old. Except for the corporate elite, the final five years to retirement are uneventful and usually a downhill slide. Sometimes the individual is moved out of a position of management to make way for the next generation. In such a case, he enters a pool of workers (*buzuki*) that are attached in one shape or form to larger groups or performs piecemeal work.

The kind of corporate culture we've looked at here tends to be quite frustrating to westerners, and for several reasons. First, the age of the person with whom you are talking is often of paramount importance. The younger the person, the more likely the prevailing Japanese hierarchy has not attached a great deal of importance to him. The young man will be ignored. Should you be dealing with very junior staff—say, employees in their 30s—you may want to reassess what your goals are and hold out for a more senior liaison. This is especially true when you are nearing the final stages of the process. No Japanese can make a move without the expressed consent of their board or, at the very least, by a representative director. If this person fails to attend, even for a short period of time, and your perception is that your meetings are in the final rounds, there is some cause for concern.

Another confusing thing for westerners is identifying who is actually the decision maker. Since they are all promoted at or nearly at the same age, you have a plethora of people running around with the word "manager" printed on their business cards. Furthermore, the names of the groups with which you are dealing all seem to have the same name. Something, something, something "Planning."

Close scrutiny of the titles can often lead to the discovery of very, very small differences in titles. For example, Manager, Research Planning Group is a bit different than Manager, Research Planning Administration. In all likelihood, these are groups of one or two people and the manager manages only himself and his workload. The closest we have to this in the west is the rank structure of the armed forces. The Japanese hierarchy resembles the non-commissioned officer ranks to some extent. Time in grade and time in service are the most important factors to determine if you are in an eligible zone for promotion. Other factors such as a promotion interview scores and availability of slots also play major roles. As with the military where some sergeants are in positions of leadership (team leaders, squad leaders, platoon sergeant, first sergeants, etc) while others are in a support or technical role (medical, administrative, law enforcement, communications), the Japanese all receive the same pay and the same privileges when they are at the same level regardless of job function.

The workplaces in Japan differ much the same as they do in the States. Some places are wide open while other employ cubicles. By and large, and under the guise of facilitating an open transfer of information, an open venue is commonly used. Long rows of narrow desks are jammed packed onto every floor. As a matter of hierarchy, the most important people always sit next to the windows, while the least important person sits as far away from the window as is possible. Even walking into an empty room, one can gauge importance—or at least the longevity of service—by the type of chair the desk possesses. Very junior employees have low-backed chairs with no arms. As you move up, elements are added to the chair. First arms, then a higher back, then, for the upper echelon, chairs that are unique unto themselves.

Desks, too, have their place in importance. The lowest ranking people will have desks that may have been literally sold at police auctions. These desks are reputed to be the smallest desks anywhere in the world. As you increase in importance, your desk also improves in quality until finally you arrive at something on par with what western executives are accustom.

The daily work environment at a typical office building can be quite variable. Oftentimes it is reminiscent of a graveyard, and employees labor in funeral parlor silence much of the time. There is some cross conversation but it usually is restricted to business.

Just as age equates to intellect, time equates to productivity. The average official Japanese workday is eight-and-a-half to nine hours not including an hour for lunch. Few workers heed that, though. They usually arrive early—anywhere from one and a half hours to thirty minutes early—and leave late, on the order of no less than one hour later. It is not uncommon to put in two to three hours of overtime every day. Combine this with an average commute time of one to two hours and it makes for a very long business day. Not that anything gets accomplished through the overtime. Many workers just sit at their desks and wait for their manager to go home so as to give the appearance of having a good work ethic.

An interesting aside: This influences why Japan does not use daylight savings time. The "official reason" is because the government insists that changing all the timetables twice yearly for the intricate domestic transportation systems would cause a great number of problems. But the train systems—receiving far more use than any other domestic system—already change periodically and there never seems to be any problems. Daylight savings time would prove onerous though: Few businessmen will return home while it is still light outside. Just like a dairy cow coming in from the pastures at night, going home in darkness has been ingrained in Japanese salarymen for so long that it is borders on Pavlovian.

Island Thinking

Japan has always gone out of its way to remain as isolated as possible from the rest of the world. This isolation is considerably different from the Monroe Doctrine practiced by the United States for the better part of the 19th century. In the latter case, at least, there was an influx of peoples and cultures and the nation was not cutoff from the rest of the world entirely. America simply chose not to get involved with the affairs of other nations. Japan, on the other hand, wanted nothing more than to create its own microcosm with sterile boundaries permitting nothing to enter or exit.

Perhaps this was a ploy by the power brokers of the time to isolate Japan thereby leaving the general populace easy prey for whatever conditioning those in control deemed fit. Or perhaps it was from a genuine desire to preserve and keep pure a culture that, from an insider's point of view, transcended all other known cultures of the time. At the end of the day, it doesn't really matter which, what is important is the impact this policy had on the mindset of the people.

No one really likes to admit that they aren't who they think they are. Everyone can relate to that. All of us at one time or another think we are the person we construct in our minds when, in reality, we are who others perceive us to be. Without that epiphany, there can be no behavioral changes outside to match what we believe is inside. The Japanese are no different in this respect save for the fact that they haven't arrived at that moment of reconciliation.

This self-realization comes from living in an environment where the norms are constantly challenged and redefined. In the west, we are the product of two defining eras in Earth's history: the Protestant Reformation and the Age of Enlightenment. This has imbued us with a critical and analytical mindset that makes us believe that anything is possible. It also broadened our horizons. A major impetus of both these events was the close proximity of vastly differing people.

The Japanese experienced none of this on the epic scale that we have, and their historic chance encounters with change and things different, drove them to live as shut-ins. The result: Island Thinking.

Out-to-Get-Me

During the Edo Period (1602 – 1868) the only port that was open to foreigners was Nagasaki. The newly and self-proclaimed *shogun*, Tokugawa Ieyasu, saw the inherent dangers of new ideas and the lure of strange, exotic customs. But mostly, he was concerned that the ideas of freedom and liberty could be used as lever to wrest from him all his hard-earned power. One thing was for certain, however: He wasn't going to chance foreign ideas, influences, or powers to corrupt the Japan he united and was in the process of re-building. So, to preempt any unrest, he herded up all the foreigners and either deported them or killed them along with any of his own people that were sympathizers. Many, uncountable Japanese Christians died in this purge.

But Tokugawa did have some thought to the fact that he lived on a relatively barren island devoid of some natural resources that were abundantly found in other lands. In some respects, the Japanese, as today, relied heavily on trading with foreign countries in order to maintain a healthy supply of raw materials that would be fashioned into the tools and toys of the elite. This, then, was a major factor in Tokugawa allowing one port in all of Japan to be open to foreigners. Foreigners—mainly the Portuguese—were allowed access to a small portion of the city of Nagasaki. No foreigner was permitted to actually set foot on the mainland though they were afforded the luxury of being able to take R&R on a small island just off shore. The penalties for entering Japan proper were severe and swift. Not many trespassers survived such an incident.

Thus began a long period of isolation that would only end with the advent of Commodore Perry and his Black Ships. Even then, as the age of the samurai was fading and the age of the businessman was dawning, liaisons from the Japanese government to foreign interests were careful to throw up all kinds of sundry hurdles and walls to baffle the foreigners as to process and procedure, and to keep them in the dark as to decision-making.

This all seems to be a bit overly protectionist in its approach, but Japanese have ingrained in themselves a uniquely overriding fear of invasion. Again, it boils down to a perceived loss of power. By hook or by crook, they have always manipulated situations to maintain the *status quo*. One reason why it has been traditionally so hard to enter the Japanese market is because the government has done all it can to ensure that no foreigner nor foreign entity could ever displace a Japanese as an executive, gain control over a Japanese firm, or usurp an industrial sector.

No matter how big or how small a Japanese corporation is today, if they are involved with a foreign company and that foreign company manages to exploit a deal, or if the foreign company just plain and simple out-negotiates a Japanese company, the perception inside the Japanese company is that the foreigners are trying to damage—or worse—destroy the company. At this point, and if the deal has yet to be signed off, a foreign company can expect to encounter a barrage of tactics which amount to re-posturing. The Japanese company feels it needs to exact some last-minute concessions—however weird and irrelevant—from its potential partner in order to achieve an acceptable measure of equality.

And this is where the "saving face" expression comes into play. Everyone has heard of this expression. To the Japanese, saving face is meant as a soft landing for a mistake or misconception. In this way, everyone stays on equal ground and everyone keeps their pride intact. To the westerner, saving face means "Make me feel good about being stupid." And it seems to be done in negotiations through a *quid pro quo*. In this way, there is no obvious or perceived weakness or ineptitude or anything else that would indicate to the world at large that this individual—and by extension the company—lacks business savvy and was too inexperienced to conduct business in the international arena.

But as Americans, though, we believe, and with no small amount of rational justification, that to the victors belong the spoils. You don't get what you deserve, you get what you negotiate. How many times has a businessman repeated that mantra to himself as he prepares for the battle that we have come to know as international business? We don't break our backs trying to get the best deal for our respective companies only to give points away in the end so the other side can feel better about themselves.

But the Japanese will expect that of you. So, as you are waiting for the final draft of the contract to clear the approval process, you may want to decide what bones you can throw that have little or no impact on your bottom line but are flashy enough to earn your Japanese counterpart some kudos from his management. This, of course, depends on the position of power from which you are negotiating, but by and large, it's something with which you likely will be confronted.

The paranoia harbored by Japanese companies is not always readily observable by western business collaborators. Fear not, it is there, and it may manifest itself in any one of ways. The single most obvious is when a response to your proposal seems way out of line with the events that have transpired to date. Another is when a severely limiting and restrictive clause is interjected into an otherwise sensible document. This clause generally puts constraints on what you can and cannot do. It is their price of moving forward. To them, your acceptance of such a clause defines the degree of interest you have and demonstrates to them your "commitment."

When you hold the upper hand in business deals, every action, every word, every nuance could be viewed as a conspiratorial one. It may be obvious; it may not be. As you walk down the path towards a successful deal, keep in mind that the Japanese samurai sword is a single-edged weapon for a reason. It only can cut one way.

A Secret Society

For all its socialization and reliance on group consensus in decision-making, Japan is overtly a very tight-lipped culture. Within an organization, each group (*bu*) is isolated from the others, much like an island unto itself. The spread of information between groups is very controlled and employees are careful about what bits of information are allowed to leave their group. This seems to fly in the face of their reputation as a consensus driven machine. It is not. While in the west we rely on clear lines of hierarchy, authority and power, the Japanese focus on cooperation. They are equally reliant on lines of authority and seats of power, but they are far, far more subtle about it.

By keeping secrets from one another, even the smallest and most insignificant group can retain some stature of power. Often it is enough for a manager to chime in once at a large corporate meeting to keep himself in the spotlight. As long as the piece of the puzzle he holds has some fundamental importance, he can hold a project ransom. These are the hard politics of intra-group competition.

Despite their "togetherness," every Japanese manager wants to be known as the man who saved the company. They want to be responsible for the deal of the century. A superhero. To this end, they hold back critical pieces of information from the foot soldiers and only supply these tidbits when the business team is devoid of hope and when the exposure to them is a high profile one. To be seen as humbly swooping in and saving the day can often guarantee a manager's continued importance and access to senior management.

It is not uncommon for the right hand not to know what the left hand is doing. This can lead to two parts of the same company unwittingly competing against each other for the same thing. Often times this competition is not realized until after the deal is sealed. Yet, despite these flounderings, there are no evident moves in Japanese companies to become more transparent. To do so would be to expose each functional group for what is really is—or isn't. Because of the abundance of managers, each one needs to have some perception of power in his job. His goal is to avoid the salary drop at 55 and to retain the appearance of importance throughout his tenure with the company.

Part of the secrecy perceived by westerners is rooted in the basic fundamentals of the language itself. Japanese have been termed a "high context" people; that is, they do not require a great deal of verbalization to be understood, and each word they say is imbued with a host of meanings and nuances. Largely, this is due to being of a single race and that race being subjected to the boundaries imposed by the sea. It's something like growing up in a family with a great many siblings. You all know what each other are thinking without the need for lengthy explanations. The entire Japanese society is part of a collective consciousness. Abbreviated questions are answered by grunts that, to the inquisitor, provide a clear answer but to a casual bystander looks as though two great apes are discoursing. Even in sentence structure, subjects are often omitted and it is left up to the listener to "fill-in the gaps."

But make no mistake about it. If the Japanese keep secrets from one another when they are in the same company, you can be sure that a great number of things will be held back from you. The trick is finding the right key to unlock the truth. It's kind of like peeling an onion. You need to strip away layer after layer before arriving at the core. This concept so penetrates the Japanese culture that they even have special names associated with it. The superficial truth is called the "*tatamai*." It's not exactly a lie, but it's not exactly the truth, either. It is some excuse that is being fronted to avoid disclosing the real reason behind an action, policy, or proposal. That real reason is what the Japanese refer to as the "*hone*." If you really want to unsettle your Japanese counterpart in a negotiation, ask him sometime if the reason for something is the *hone* or the *tatamai*. That person will never look at you the same again.

And from what strata you begin in your efforts to find the truth in the corporate hierarchy depends on the number of layers you need to sort through before arriving at the truth. Take solace in knowing that this is irrelevant of whether you are a foreigner or a native. As a foreigner, you'll need to do a bit more sorting, but even employees of the same company face similar barriers. One difference is that Japanese employees frequently take at face value the first story they are told. It is not that they believe it, but that it isn't their place to question the source especially if it comes from an older employee.

But as a westerner, you are bred from the time you were three years old to ask the question, "Why." Reasons are the key to our way of thinking. We try to keep to some semblance of logic and to do that, we require a train of thought connecting all the dots beginning with the premise and ending with the conclusion. Not so in Japan. But your "why" can serve as a cultural potato peeler. If you are persistent enough, and if the illogic of the explanations given to you are laid open in a simple and obvious manner, you will eventually arrive at the truth.

Or not. Part of being a secret society is never letting on to what you know—or don't know. The latter case is the more frightening of the two when engaged in business negotiations. It is not beyond a Japanese businessman to—how should I put this—enliven the proceedings with a creative aura. Technically put, they improvise. They really don't know the answer, but because they want to give you the impression that they are important enough to be privy to the information that you require, they may make something up.

The take home point here is to keep this phrase in your back pocket at all times: "How do you know?" Nothing will derail a conversation as quickly as this, particularly if you believe you are being taken down the mulberry road. Chances are they don't know…and neither does anyone else in their company. Be careful how you react to that. It may not be their fault. It is possible, and even likely, that they have accepted some *tatamai* as the gospel truth and are acting upon that when, in fact, that piece of information is incongruent with your sense of logic.

A permutation of this is that should your counterpart not answer the question because he does not know, you may experience what the Native Americans called the "long drink of silence." While he simply does not know because *he* never asked, the asking on your part inevitably leads to an embarrassing situation. And so he finds himself in the middle of uncertainty. His processor locks up and can't seem to move on to the next step, or simply can't move, period. Especially if vocalization is required. It is prudent to gauge how far to push that situation. Go too far and you risk damaging your future relationship with this individual with whom, presumably, you will have to seal the deal.

But if you don't push enough, there will be a void in your information database and this can hardly lead to an informed and intelligent decision. Balance is the key, and there is no firm and fast rule to knowing where and when to stop the pursuit. One rule of thumb, however, is if your core temperature rises above 98.6 degrees Fahrenheit, stop. Anything that can betray frustration—and there will be frustration—is like an exit ramp sign on the highway. Take a physical break from the meeting. This will help re-center your emotions and, perhaps, offer the Japanese negotiator the time he needs to find the answer. Or it may allow him to come up with another, alternative scenario that he thinks will carry the day.

Although omission of information can often be the basis and bias for a perceived lie, by far the biggest reason is a misunderstanding of English. Your Japanese counterpart asks question A, you give straightforward reply B, and he relates X to his management. Later if the error is discovered, usually in print form somewhere, the "lie" word will be used in the Japanese decision-making circles. It can be a matter of the listener hearing what he wants to hear and not what message is actually being transmitted, or the listener having some pre-conceived expectations and making the response fit into that, or the listener is plain and simple not good at English.

To avoid this frustration it is important to always speak with clarity and using as many one syllable words as possible. This, of course, is an exaggeration. Avoid using idiomatic expressions when answering critical questions, stay away from negative constructs ("isn't it", "aren't you", etc.) and use simple grammar and language. These are key in being viewed as an honest broker. Using colloquialisms will almost certainly result in the Japanese having no idea of what you said. Embarrassment will prevent them from asking you to elaborate on everything after "Let me briefly explain."

Americans tend to lean towards over-explaining and that leads to lengthy tirades. You can be sure your Japanese counterparts will not understand all this and even if they could, would not care. For them the result is primary; any underlying reasons are secondary. The tendency to wax poetic is further enhanced by the fact that the Japanese display polar opposite behavior. They typically remain silent. This serves as encouragement for the western to keep talking. "They must not understand what I'm saying, so I'll explain it again, and again, and again, *ad nauseam*," goes the thinking.

In such instances, the inevitable happens: you say too much. Whether you disclose a detail you were hoping to save for later or you open up a whole new can of worms by making a connection to a new but distantly related point, the course of the discussion along with its tone will be irreversibly changed. I hesitate to say "damaged," although that, too, is a possibility. The deal will take on an unexpected twist that you may find hard from which to extricate yourself. The best advice here is to learn to be comfortable with long periods of silence. We tend to look at these times as "trouble" or an interruption in the flow. In the Japanese arena, they are not. Quiet times are for reflection on what has been said. They are trying to figure out what you said, what it means, and the best way to reply. Remember, this is a second language for them. Processing time is important and they will speak when they are ready. From their response you'll be able to gauge the cause of the deep well of silence. On the other hand, be wary of silences that last too awfully long; especially, if they seem fixated on the ceiling or are mulling things over with their eyes closed.

It can be difficult for Americans to sort the wheat from the chafe when it comes to Japanese transparency. Even at the national level, countries have been pushing the Japanese to make their systems more open. But the Japanese have resisted these moves. Becoming more transparent means that everyone can understand the process, partake in it, and profit from it. Again, the fear is that Japanese will lose control and power in their own back yard. Imperialism will rear its ugly head and the western hordes will be landing on the shores of Honshu by the boatloads. There will be no recourse for the small to medium Japanese companies. Unemployment rates will soar, inflation will skyrocket, and the burden on the national government will be overly onerous. Japan will be exploited and hen discarded when there is nothing more to extract from the economy.

By holding back information, the Japanese side retains an ace in the hole to play whenever they think they are getting steamrolled. Usually, it's delivered with a crescendo, wrecking the plans and progress that took hours, or days to construct.

Ferreting out all the crucial data during interactions with the Japanese can be much liking pulling teeth. They do not want to show their entire hand; a wise and natural policy for anyone when embarking on any business deal. But when taken to these extremes, it can cross the line and gravitate towards counter productivity. They do little to let the other party know exactly what the ground rules are and little is communicated about what conditions are needed and what expectations are harbored for a successful conclusion to the business deal. In defense of the Japanese negotiator, the senior management may not have clearly elucidated what they, corporately, are seeking. Or they may simply not know themselves. This is another very real possibility.

Secrecy can be, and often is, a convenient cover for ignorance. By "not disclosing" a piece of information "at this time," raises the question in the minds of the other party as to whether or not the individual actual knows the answer or if he is simply playing his cards close to his chest. This occurs both with internal discussions at Japanese companies as well as with outside parties. To get what you want, it sometimes is better not to tip your hand too soon. But, if the question or request for information is relatively routine and benign, and your counterpart hesitates to volunteer an appropriate reply, you can be reasonably sure that you'll be needing to put this on the table again later on.

Secrets always contain a measure of power. Keeping them from individuals who need them to perform is to exercise power over them. It is also something to fall back on if you are being out-maneuvered. From a Japanese perspective, the keeping of secrets and the dissemination of information on a "need to know" basis is their way to ensure that no one, single person has too much power. Full disclosure would serve to marginalize the functions of other members of the group and where ten people were necessary before, full disclosure can relegate that number to two or three. This leaves seven or eight people with little more to do than sit in a corner twiddling their thumbs. Naturally, this abrades the Japanese socialist sensibilities: People of the same age are essentially the same in standing; no one person is superior to another. This all falls apart if all the pieces of the puzzle are gathered in one place only to find out they are easily managed by a small number people. A great number of senior managers would find themselves redundant.

The Japanese also use secrecy as a hedge against panic. It is the card played by senior management to curb the emotions of their feudal subjects. This is especially the case when there is a major shift in corporate structure or policy. I'm not sure where this school of thought originated. Japanese companies still promote lifetime employment—at least in the larger organizations—and employees tend to blindly believe that the company will take care of them no matter what is the state of finances. But any news of M&A activities is stifled at the highest levels and those that do know, whether they are actively involved or have stumbled across it purely by happenstance, are swore to secrecy. There is a belief by management that the employees would dispair and many of the better, more talented folk would run for cover. That is, they would take advantage of having marketable abilities and move on to somewhere else.

To prevent the brain drain and a slew of suicides, information about M&A or re-structuring is so secretive that only a blood oath would be more severe in its confidentiality provisions and consequences in breaches thereof. When the news finally officially breaks, there has been, historically, some kind of trauma prevention program in place. The employees are absorbed albeit in positions that are mostly window seats. Then there are the gradual phase-outs of unneeded and unwanted personnel. This is normally done through early retirements. Normal attrition does serve to thin out the employee pool, but indiscriminate "De-promotion," or moving people from the weaker of the two merging units to a position of much lower rank and responsibility, is a more common technique.

Secrets drive a Japanese company like gas drives a car.

There has been a trend to become more "transparent" in business, in part spurred by the growing western presence in Japanese and the inability for these segments to clearly identify criteria and standards of day-to-day business operations. Even with this pressure building and even though the country is, to a limited extent, bowing under this pressure, it will take decades before there is a free flow of information across operating groups in a company. It will take longer for transparency to take root to the point where outside agencies—and this extends to investors as well—can really have a notion of what is actually taking place inside a blue-chip Japanese company.

First Contact

L ike everything else you undertake in business, preparation is the single most important thing in conducting business in Japan. But no matter how many of the books in bookstores or libraries you read, it is unlikely that you would—or could—be prepared for what you are about to encounter. The hard cold fact is that many of those reference books were written by people who spent only a few weeks or, at the most, a couple of years in Japan. That is not nearly enough time to penetrate the veil of Japan Inc. More often than not, these references have the same inherent value that you would get by talking to someone who had taken a few business trips to the island and was reporting to you his experiences. I don't think I'd want to hinge the success or failure of my business on that level of hearsay.

Many of the things I've read have turned out to be wrong. Not mistaken, not misquoted, not taken out of context, but plain and simply wrong. Over the past decade, I've been looking out over the other side of the table into the eyes of westerners while taking the part of the

Japanese in negotiations. It's from this perspective that I am about to offer advice. I speak in generalities and the suggestions here are by no means hard and fast rules that are a guaranteed axioms or formula for success. Each business deal is a bit different and unique unto itself. As you conduct your diligence prior to undertaking any kind of trip to Japan, or as you ramp up your efforts to enter into some relationship with a Japanese corporation, you may find that some of these insights may come in handy while some may not. No matter how you approach Japan, remember three words: Improvise. Adapt. Overcome.

Many deals begin with either a correspondence or personal visit. These may be specific or they may be cold calls. Either way, they are approached in much the same way. Naturally, you stand a slightly better chance at being granted an audience if you have something that is directly related to their business. But whatever approach you take, the question becomes: Who should I contact first? The answer to this largely depends on what you want.

Any inquiries into M&A should be taken to the highest level you can find. Remember, policies are a matter of the utmost secrecy, and the lower echelons may have no idea that senior management is seeking to divest their division. Managers—even those heading up divisions—may think everything is corporately sound. But in Japan, the last person to learn the patient is dying is the patient. If what you're looking for is a division, contact the company president. If you are dealing with a holding company structure and are looking to acquire one of its business units, contact the holding company president. Inquiries along these lines can greatly increase the chance that the answer you receive is the real answer *viz*. the truth.

In Japan, there are not many "back doors." In both the US and the EU, it is a common business practice to use networking to assist in the conduct of business. This works well in a western context and can save time. You very often get the meeting and with the right person. The reason this works is that there is a free flow of information and openness in relationships. Indeed, we have come to rely on networking to cut through some of the bureaucracy and confusion that large corporations inherently generate. But behind the rice curtain, this practice can be counterproductive. For the same reasons that this approach is so effective in the west is exactly the same reason it is not in Japan. Information is compartmentalized and guarded; not free flowing and open. Only an elite few have all the pieces of the puzzle in their possession. And they're not predisposed to sharing. Many times going through a low-level intermediary results in a loss of strategic initiative.

If you do try to network in Japan, it may be that you have a particular confidence in your source. Maybe you've downed a couple of beers with the guy at a few conferences. Maybe he lets you use his first name instead of the stiff titular "-*san*". But do not be confused where his allegiances lie. Japan is a country of façades. It needs to be since so many people live in such close proximity to one another. This makes what you see rarely what you get. You may ask your guy for a "favor," and he may agree. But have no disillusions; nothing is off the record in Japan. He will be duty bound to bring this up at some staff meeting or the other. The issue may be yanked away from him and be deliberated by a completely different functional group. Even so, he may remain the conduit through which this other group communicates. The result is that you think you are dealing with one guy in confidence when, in fact, he is just acting as a functionary shielding the identities of the people with who you really want—and need—to have a dialogue. This can go on for a long, long, LONG time before the klaxons start going off in your head and you wake-up to find that you've just spent the better part of a year talking to the wrong guy and making little progress. And as we have seen in Japanese culture, you'll likely need to start at square one again with the right guy even though he has been in the loop the whole time. Meanwhile, where are your competitors?

There is a "good 'ol boy" network, but is much better used if the good 'ol boy (OB in Japanese; literally, "Old Boy") used are ex-executives and not middle-level or upper-level management. A former president can have a great deal of influence in brokering a deal than can a former general manager of business development. There is a great institutional memory in Japan, not of things that worked, but of who people were. This is historical in the sense that the titular rulers of Japan's feudal years never actually ruled. The reigning *shogun* was merely a figurehead. He was controlled by the former shogun or a committee of lords (*bakafu*).

There is still a shadow of this system today, although the sun is slowly chasing these shadows away A former CEO or head of the board can wield a great deal of influence over the company. A game of golf with the present president along with a few "suggestions," and suddenly all the doors that were formerly closed are wide open. And so are some you didn't even know existed.

If you are like the majority of westerners and are starting at ground zero, one way to be sure that you hit the mark as early as possible is to send your business development people to conduct a "general information exchange." This is typically used to introduce your respective organization and almost always will be accompanied by the items you need most: An annual report, and an organizational chart. These exchanges can be done extemporaneously, with only two to three weeks prior notice. They take about two to two-and-a-half hours to complete, depending on the industry. The Japanese rarely turn these opportunities down unless the there is an obvious lack of synergy.

Japan, for all its electronic toys and gadgets, is by and large computer illiterate, or more accurately they lack computer savvy. The ability to operate a computer is improving across the board in Japanese companies as more and more of the video game generation takes their place in business. But let's be fair. Japan has some top contenders in the leading business sectors, whether it be life sciences, high tech or CEEM (chemical, environmental, energy and materials). These players have evolved over the years and are pretty much on par with their western competitors. One of the overarching reasons for this is that these companies have come to realize that their fortunes are made outside Japan. If they hope to be a part of that wealth, they need to mirror the successes already established in their sectors. There are rules and there are norms. Toyota, Astellas, and Sony have all immersed themselves in this olio and have fared quite well. It is in the mid-sized Japanese companies where we see the disparities of which we are discussing.

And these mid-sized companies are still waiting for their decision-making employees to catch up with information technology. Like any tool, knowing how to operate it and knowing how to apply it are two very different things. A simple test: Go to your homepage. Look at the design. Test drive it. You probably are very familiar with it and have some strong opinions on how to make it better. Now, find ten Japanese companies in your industry. Go to their homepage. Test drive that. If they are comparatively interactive and well laid out, your foray into a partnership with them should be a bit easier.

As westerners, we have come to depend on the Internet for the lion's share of our daily information. It is easy. It is convenient. And it is all there. In the pharmaceutical business, if I want to send some introductory material to the licensing group of a company, I would go to their homepage and I would almost always be able to find the correct person with whom to correspond. This taking only a matter minutes to find. Now, despite the crudeness of many of the Japanese homepages, there is almost always some e-mail address or phone number where you can make inquires. If you take this route as first contact please allow several weeks for your message to make its way into the hands of someone who can actually draft a response; you can be fairly sure that the person listed on the homepage is not the right person. More likely he is a representative of the business affairs office or an administrative contact in the business development group.

If you desire a quicker reply, you can try going the telephone route. Be prepared for some pretty rough sounding English. Also be prepared to be bounced around the company. You'll likely play phone tag with a host of people before finally connecting with the appropriate person. The probability that a secretary has enough English to forward your call is low; be ready and willing to do a lot of international dialing. Something else to keep in mind when braving the telephone with the Japanese: The smaller the company (or division) the less likely it is to have someone who is functional in the English language. Also bear in mind that telephone conversations are extremely difficult tasks even for "fluent" Japanese English speakers.

Once you get through, you will want to follow-up your conversation by e-mail. And you would be wise to do so immediately. This will help ensure that what you said and what they heard are one in the same thing. Which means you'll be asking for an e-mail address over the phone. Few things are less painful than having a Japanese e-mail address read to you. Again, it is a matter of size: the larger companies tend to follow the simpler, western custom of just using the person's name and the company's name at a dot-com address. The smaller organizations will play a different sort of game. They use "dot-co-dot-jp" suffixes. Having to hear explanations of "underbars" and "@ marks" can lead to confusion. They also can be lengthy and not make a whole lot of sense. You may want to consider, as a safety net, to give them your e-mail address and have them send you a mail. Then you can simply attach your message and hit the "Reply" button. This does involve some risk in that the person at the other end can actually understand what you are asking them to do and will actually do it.

Of course, there is the subject of your first contact which is at the heart of why you want a meting. This is important. Opportunities, in whatever form, are not completely lost on the Japanese. You may need to walk them through just what it entails and how it can globally or domestically benefit their company, but you can be sure that Japanese companies do possess a certain basic competency for realizing profitability, at least in the higher echelons of the organization.

Finally, persistence helps. If you have something that really is of interest to the industry, someone in a position of authority in a Japanese company will eventually catch on to this. You just need to find him in the crowd.

Travel, Weather and Clothes

Japan, as a country, lies in the middle of nowhere. It's just how geography worked out. This partially accounts for why it took so long to pry the doors open for trade. For the ancient mariners—the Portuguese, the Dutch, the Spanish and the English—their established trade routes put Japan at the edge of the civilized world. This really hasn't changed much since the advent of the jet airplane. Whether you are traveling from Europe or the Americas, it takes about 11 to 13 hours of air time to get there.

Japan also lies inconveniently close to the international dateline. This means that your tickets will have the dreaded "+1" on it for one of the directions you are traveling. For those who are not familiar with this notation, consider yourselves lucky. But as you are on the brink of taking your first trip of many to Japan you will become all too familiar with what it means: You lose a day in your travel. Either in coming or returning you will collide with the earth's terminator and move from day into night and then back into day. When you fly in the opposite direction you pick that day back up. From America, it takes two days to get to Japan and one day to get back. Oftentimes on the flight home you find yourself landing before you took off.

The impact of this "+1" cannot be understated. It takes three full days to travel to and from Japan. Out of a five-day work week, that's a big chunk of your time, and leaves little in the way of time on the ground. Travel inside Japan is done mostly by train, which further detracts from time spent in the meeting rooms. If you need to travel from Tokyo to Osaka, you better plan on an easy three hours on a super express bullet train (*shinkansen*) and another 30 minutes to an hour at both ends to get to anf from the train station.

A quick note on traveling by train or subway in Japan: Do not, I say again, DO NOT misplace your ticket. You need it to get out of the train station. Keep it someplace safe and where you can get to it with relative ease. Without it you will be charged from the farthest station. There can sometimes be up to four different tickets you need and without delving into the details, it is simplest to keep track of whatever you are issued at the ticket window. There is plenty of train staff at the entrance and exit turnstiles to assist you if you aren't sure how to get through or what you need. If in doubt, there is always a lane either on the far right or far left with an attendant. These guys are very well versed in helping travelers—even Japanese ones—with the complexities of the Japanese train ticketing system. Know that losing train tickets is one of the most common *faux pas* that happens to first time visitors—especially American visitors—in Japan.

But before worrying too much about mastering the

train system the few days you are in Japan, first you need to get through immigration and customs. From the US and EU, no visas are needed, but be prepared for a very crowded flight almost any day of the week. The Japanese like to travel, and the package "tours" available in Japan load people like cattle onto many of the off-peak weekly flights. Naturally, a Sunday flight will be full, but the one to really watch for is the Saturday flights. A Saturday flight from the US, as typically scheduled, will put you on the ground in Japan late Sunday afternoon. Most flights from the US touch down between 2 and 5 pm. This means you can be ready for business Monday morning. This also means that Saturday flights are most attractive to business people and many will be vying for seating on those flights.

Travel relaxed. That is, don't walk onto the plane in your suit unless you plan to go directly into a meeting when you land. It is a long and cramped flight, so it's best to be comfortable. With this said, don't sport the grunge look either. You will want to maintain a very respectable and tidy appearance for the sake of the law enforcement gentlemen waiting for you at customs and immigration. You will already stand out in a crowd, either by height, weight, or hair color. You already are a target for custom officials. By being groomed, and well attired, you can avoid the suspicions cast on those arriving disheveled and poorly dressed. By presenting themselves in such a fashion, these people are inviting extensive searches and questioning that will significantly delay clearing customs and immigration.

As for what constitutes "appropriate" dress, it varies. Cargo pants are acceptable provided that they are a solid color and not unduly wrinkled. Holes in any clothing will immediately flag you as some Dead-head dope-smoker. For women, casual dress such as blue jeans is fine, but—and although you may see Japanese women dressed "questionably" by US standards—it is best not to opt for anything too risqué. They may feel your purpose of visit is of another kind of business. The traveler's dress code to Japan can be summarized by three words: Clean. Conservative. Respectable.

This all sounds a bit melodramatic, but remember that you are entering a country that has spent all its history trying to keep people out. Westerners do get turned away from immigration and some people do get stopped at customs. The typical questions of where you came from, how long you plan to stay, what is the nature of your visit, and presenting a return ticket are usually the only ones you'll get asked. But as a foreigner, you have a better than even odds chance that you will be asked to open your bags and that they will be rifled through by the customs officer. This is especially true if this is your first visit to Japan. Some seedier looking westerners are invited to a back room where a more intense and time-consuming search and questioning takes place. A prior visit to Japan in your passport greatly alleviates the chances of this happening.

Facial hair is still a bit rough for Japanese to handle, although not to the extent it was once. Moustaches and beards should be neatly groomed and trimmed, or else prepare yourself for a one-to-two-hour backroom affair. If you do sport one or the other or both, smile a lot. Foreigners with beards and moustaches do not invoke images of a congenial figure. Combined with size and, often enough, shape, it reminds them of something very,

very different. A smile can break up these dreaded features and help put the Japanese at ease. Smiles, in general are used by Japanese to cover all kinds of situations.

Like America, virtually all the major international airports lie far outside the cities they represent. The major difference is that transportation to and from the city is particularly tiresome. There will inevitably be train service from the airport and there is always a semi-competent English speaking Japanese attendant at the ticket counters of almost any service. Trains are by far the cheapest mode, but sometimes you can luck out and catch a shuttle bus that services your hotel or place of final destination. Beware, the drivers don't speak much English, but they can get you to where you need to go. The basic rule when traveling to and from airport is that what you gain in savings you generally lose in time.

Your choice of hotels, as a westerner, is limited. Limited in the sense that you probably want something that fits your idea of a hotel. Or just plain fits. Japan is replete with "business hotels" which are to the Japanese businessman what a Super 8 is to an American businessman. That's about where the comparison stops. It comes down to a matter of scale. The business hotel room, at roughly between $100 - $200 a night, is about the size of a federal prison cell. Westerners of average height often are too tall for the bed, and literally have to exit the unit bathroom to turn around. My recommendation is to stick the larger, reputable international hotels. In Tokyo you have the Imperial Hotel (*Teikoku*), the Okura, the New Otani Hotel, and the Palace Hotel, to name a few. These are very expensive, on the order of $200 - $275 per night, but cater more to the foreign crowd. This means that English is not going to be a problem, that the amenities are more along the lines those that you are accustom—and that they are readily available. You needn't worry about being served culinary mysteries. Furthermore, even though the taxi drivers don't speak a syllable of English, they recognize the names of this class of hotel and can get you there without any lengthy explanations. Staying at business hotels will require you to give detailed instructions on account that they are located in the backwaters of cities and that city streets rarely have any names.

After bedding down for the night and waking relatively refreshed albeit a bit disoriented, you're ready to head off to the meeting. What to wear, what to wear. This all depends on the season. Summers, the period of time covering late May until mid-September, are flush in heat and humidity. Often the numbers are the same: 90°F and 90% relative humidity. For most westerners this is oppressive, to say the least. To complicate matters, the Japanese are signators of the Kyoto Accord and actually try to do their part to meet their emission quotas. Part of this is setting the office air conditioners at 28°C (82.4°F). This can be pretty stifling when wearing a grey wool pinstripe. On the other hand, there are cases where the meeting rooms are set at 20°C, frigid compared to the outside temperature.

Autumns are the most comfortable, resembling late summer in the northeast US. Even though the mornings and nights are cool, they do not warrant overcoats. This season, as such, can extend to the New Year and a bit beyond. In the Kanto region, where Tokyo is located, it rarely drops below freezing, making "winter" suits, by US standards, unnecessary. Naturally the northern regions are snowy and winter does appear there in earnest, but to put things in perspective, the upper tip of Hokkaido, the northern most island, lies at the same latitude as Portland, Oregon in the US and Bordeaux, France in the EU.

Like many tropical and sub-tropical countries, Japan has a rainy season. This is about six weeks long beginning in early June and finishing mid-July. Typhoons are also prevalent with the majority coming at the beginning of summer and the balance at end of summer. The latter period corresponds closely to hurricane season in the US. As a note of interest, a typhoon is a baby hurricane. It possesses winds on a much smaller scale, although the rainfall may approach that of a hurricane.

Japan is an umbrella society. On rainy days or days that threaten precipitation, nearly every soul leaving the safety of their own homes will be toting an umbrella. Showers come quickly and, sometimes, violently, but rarely have lasting power. Rainfall in Japan is voluminous and can soak you to the bone in a matter of seconds. Thus the "mad dash" we are so infamous for in the US will have disastrous results in Japan. Umbrellas can be purchased nearly anywhere on rainy days, with sales stands suddenly appearing outside of train stations and inside convenient stores. The going price for an average quality umbrella is about ¥500 - ¥1000 (less than $10). If you are a high-speed business traveler, you may wish to opt for the state-of-art trifold umbrella. Quite compact, it can easily fit inside your briefcase. This accomplishes two things: first, it is secure and not likely to be pilfered; umbrellas are neck-in-neck with bicycles as items most frequently stolen. Second, it is easily handled as compared with a long stick-like thing that needs to be leverage in and out of taxicabs, on trains and through office buildings. Being stashed safely away in your attaché case eliminates the worries of losing it or trying to wield it through a city of 12 million people like some unsheathed modern-day samurai sword.

Many Japanese carry small cotton towels. Aside from being handy in the public toilets—where there are usually no paper towels or air dryers—they are indispensable in the summer months for mopping up rivers of swear that uncontrollably roll down your face, neck and arms. A small handkerchief is just not going to be enough to staunch this flow.

A few comments about accessorizing: Almost everyone knows of the no-shoes culture. If one thing has been fairly accurately depicted in the west, it's this. What is lost on most of us is what a pain in the neck it is to keep taking off and putting on our shoes. We generally do this once a day and then with the assistance of a chair and shoehorn. We don't have to do this every time we get up to go to the bathroom. In most companies, shoes are the fashion for every part of the office building. However, if you move from a city office setting to a rural research setting, this may all change. You find yourself putting on slippers to walk around the building. You have an additional burden in that you need to change the type of slipper you wear when you decide to trot off to the lavatories. Japanese restaurants present real challenges to the no shoe culture. In the rooms with mats (*tatami*), you'll need to remove your shoes. When you leave to go to the rest room, you'll need to put them on. The Japanese, who have been at this a real long, long time, have adopted a habit of buying shoes that are slightly too big for them. These they tie the same as ordinary shoes, but loosely enough where they can slip their feet in and out without much fuss.

Throughout all the shoes on shoes off ordeals, remember to always have socks without holes. Sporting holey socks is considered a huge embarrassment. If you are a single male, it is within the bounds of forgiveness albeit you will be viewed as an inept. If you are a married man, the shame is not yours but falls on your wife. In Japan, the housewife is responsible for making sure that her husband is attired in a fashion commensurate with his position. She typically spends a lot of time to ensure there are no wrinkles in shirts, spots on ties, scuff marks on shoes, and no holes in socks. Such is the mindset of Japanese that they cannot wrap their heads around the fact that this role is reversed in the west *viz.* the men generally take responsibility for their business appearance.

General meeting attire is no different than if you were visiting any other company in the world. Pressed and clean shirts pin striped grey suit, conservative tie—perhaps a red paisley or regimental but always remember blue is the color the Japanese associate with cooperation—and shined shoes. In recent years, business casual has become more and more acceptable. If in doubt, either set the dress code yourself or ask what they prefer. Remember a morning shower, which can go unsaid if you're in Japan during the summer months, a good toilet and minty fresh breath, and you're on your way. The best way to think about this, especially if it's your first time, is to think of it as a job interview. I'm not saying that you show up with hat in hand, but that you dress the part. Japanese are hypocritical, for the most part, in their view of first impressions. A lot of what they think of you comes from their first glance. Inversely, try not to do the book-and-cover-thing when you first make personal contact. Oftentimes the frumpy looking ones—particularly the scientists—are the most brilliant.

It is hard to imagine that any foreigner would feign to appear differently in Japan than anywhere else. The main problems you confront in Japan are the comparatively extreme heat and rain. Both are relentless and wipe out a one-hour toilet in a heartbeat.

Face-to-Face at Last

Meeting for the first time can be a bit confusing, what with the attempts at bowing and handshaking. It can be a real awkward moment as the westerners attempt to become Japanese and the Japanese try to become westerners. From the outside looking in, neither plays the role very well, and it all comes off as a bit comical. If you really want to join in the bowing thing, practice and get it right.

It goes something like this:

Take out your business card and, with the writing facing the receiver, grasp it ever so gently by the upper most corners using your thumb and index finger of both hands. Naturally, left hand right corner, right hand left corner (remember, it's upside-down). Hold it at chest level with your arms relaxed and slightly bent, nominally at a -15 degree angle off horizontal while angling the face of the card on a plane parallel to the receiver's eyes. Your elbows should be somewhere between your waist and sternum. Bow from the waist—not the head or shoulders—with your back rigid. The depth and duration of the bow determine the extent of respect for the person you are meeting. A neutral bow will be for approximately as long as it takes to say what you have to say and not extend beyond a 30-to-45-degree angle from the vertical. Your head should maintain eye contact. As you do so, you'll need to mutter the words "(name of your company") *no* (your last name) *to mo shimasu. Hajimemashite, yoroshiku onegaishimasu.*" Keep in mind that at the same time your Japanese counterpart will be engaging in the same thing. If you go first, the above procedure is fine. If you go second, begin with the words "*kochira koso.*" Read it silently. The amount of time you look at it equals the respect the giver perceives. Take your opposite's business card in a similar manner you have handed him yours; that is, with the thumbs and index finger of both hands and extend this into a polite bow. When waiting for someone to hand you his business card, you should be roughly at the position of "relaxed" attention. Repeat this until you've met (*aisatsu*) all the attendees.

Most of you have likely decided not to go this route. I don't blame you. Even envisioning this in your head is a bit tough. Personally, I would recommend attempting this process only after you've become more accustomed with Japan and have a better feel for both the language and customs. If you've seen it done a few dozen times, it sure makes doing it a whole lot easier.

Don't fall into the trap that ensnares many westerners who do business in Japan. They forget that they are, after all, a westerner. Present yourself that way, at least at first. Hand your business card over as you would in any other business situation. If you feel the need to "bow," a shallow perfunctory nod often suffices. Know with the greatest deal of certainty that even if you do business for a hundred years in Japan, the Japanese will always think of you as a westerner. Your manners may improve, but you will still and always be an outsider.

A couple of notes on business cards. Japan is a culture driven by business cards. Even ordinary people not engaged in business have business cards. One of the most common mistakes experienced by foreign visitors is that they fail to bring enough cards with them. Even if you've met someone before, it is likely that you will be exchanging cards with him again. The reason for this is that the names of business groups and the positions of individuals change frequently, and he will feel obligate to showcase his new "identity" to you. A rule of thumb is to estimate how many people, in total, you are scheduled to meet and double that number. And double it again. This still may have you running out. This is an embarrassment that can be avoided with a little prior planning. Even if you end up printing too many, this is better than having to decide who gets a card and who does not as you run short. It's better to have it and not need it than to need it and not have it.

The question often arises as to whether or not to have special "Japanese" business cards printed up. The common practice when doing this is to have your usual business card on one side and the Japanese transliteration on the other. Recently, some business cards have a mix of languages on one side, leaving the other free for note taking. The choice of which to use is entirely up to you, but the double-sided card still seems to be the standard and often the Japanese instinctively flip it over to see what is written on the other side. A card with dual languages is not a must; it is a matter of personal preference. One thing to be wary of, however, is how you are represented on the Japanese side. Before you have a ton of the things printed up, take the prototype card and check it with a Japanese speaker, or reader in this case. Even this is a bit dicey if that person does not have any experience with business. The average Japanese speaker may not know how to distinguish between the different levels of management in a Japanese company. The best advice is to seek out a reputable translation company.

Representing your name in Japanese can also be mission impossible. Never, never attempt to take the syllables of your name and render them in Chinese characters (*kanji*). The result provides endless hours of amusement for native Japanese and a perpetual state of embarrassment for you. Japanese names, like English names, have specific combinations of kanji leading to specific meanings and if you go down this road and write your name in kanji, it will appear to the native speakers as jibberish. Case in point: My name in Japanese is pronounced Ma-aku. A representative *kanji* is 真悪. While the pronunciation is accurate, the ideographs mean "true evil." It's not something I want in an introduction to potential partners as I try to convince them of a mutually profitable busies deal. The Japanese syllabary used to write foreign words is "katakana." It contains block-like symbols that represent the 55 spoken syllables in the Japanese language. Using these symbols, your name is spelled as it pronounced—not as you would pronounce it, but as a native Japanese speaker would. Since the Japanese phonetic alphabet consists of a single vowel, or a consonant-vowel combination where the consonant is relegated to k, s, t, n, h, m, y (only *ya*, *yu*, and *yo*), r, and w (only *wa*), and since there are no equivalents to many English sounds—predominantly of which are th, l, r, v and soft c, and since it is impossible to pronounce correctly double consonant sounds without introducing a vowel, some names can be butchered in the translation. For example, the words "nation" and "Nathan" may be indiscriminate to a native speaker's ear. Any American of Polish, Russian, or Eastern Europe descent would be hard pressed to recognize their names. So once the transliteration has been done, you, again, may want to search out a Japanese person in the States that can read kana. They will be able to tell you if what is written on your card remotely mirrors your name. What you want to steer clear of is trying to do this on your own. Even if you are well-versed in kana, the chances of you actually getting the standard katakana spelling of your name remains slim. There is a tendency to transliterate each syllable when that is not always necessary. For example, an uninitiated would spell my name マルク (Ma-ru-ku) in an attempt to incorporate all the roman letters, when in fact it is spelled マーク (Ma a ku), and pronounced as if one was from Boston: Maaak.

As far as order and orientation are concerned, order should be as it would appear if you were writing a western style business card: first name, middle initial, last name. Initials should be left as Roman letters. So, James T. Kirk would be ジェムス T. カーク (Jaymusu T. Kaaku). It doesn't really matter if you prefer to run your information lengthwise down the card or the more traditional width-wise, so long as the front and back match. I don't recommend mixing or matching style only because the Japanese may use the one side of the card as a comparative reference for reading the other.

In the States, we treat business cards given to us as, well, little slips of paper with stuff written on it. In Japan, business card etiquette is a bit different. Actually, very different. Business cards (*meishi*), are treated in accordance with how you would treat the person. In this day and age, it may be a well-circulated story that you never pocket Japanese business cards in your pants pocket or lazily toss them to one side, or stuff them carelessly into a daily planner. Generally, it is a good idea to lay the cards out in front of you, in an alignment that corresponds with the seating of their donors. This does two things: first you are showing respect and good manners; second, it helps you remember the names, which, if this is your first time, may be a little difficult.

When finished, pocket the cards in either your shirt pocket or inside breast pocket of your jacket. Alternatively, you can put them in your own cardholder as long as this item is not normally kept in your pants pocket.

Being a westerner and already deciding you won't put yourself through the Japanese custom of introduction, you settle on a handshake and a smile to accompany your business card. Just as it is awkward for Americans to do the bowing thing, few Japanese have ever really become comfortable with the handshake thing. Their handshakes tend to be too limp and last forever. We, as Americans, have been so inured to the firm, three-second handshake that we never have thought about how to extricate ourselves from someone who won't let go. Then there's the oft-encountered "pulsing" handshake, where the other person squeezes your hand in an undulating fashion.

For the first meeting, it may be the best idea to keep your self-introduction as is; that is, present yourself as you would to the company down the street. On subsequent visits, if they materialize, you can inch your way to being more "Japanese." And, indeed, with the Japanese focus on relationships, this would be advisable, as it would project the image of respecting the customs and traditions of Japan. This will serve to strengthen your ties with that company. Not a bad idea especially if you are engaged in a competitive situation.

Throughout this part of the first meeting, keep in mind that for everything that may seem unorthodox to you there will be an equal number of things that strike your Japanese counterpart in the same way. Simply by virtue of being small- to mid-sized, they lack the experience with international firms that the bigger companies may have. But this is a generality for there are some of large (by Japanese standards) companies that are equally if not more inexperienced at international business. The frequent cycling of employees throughout a string of internal jobs is a major contributing factor. With this type of system there is little in the way of establishing institutional memory, and they are constantly reinventing the wheel every five years or so when job rotations take place.

You're ready to take your seat, but where is the best place to sit? In Japan there is an unwritten rule about who sits where. It is easy to tell the hierarchy of any meeting merely by looking at the position of everyone in the room. Using the main entrance to the room as a reference, the home team sits closest the door and the away team sits opposite. On either particular side, the most important person is situated in the center; the ends of the table are rarely used. This is consistent with both the socialist psyche of Japan as a country and the idea of consensus as a decision-making tool in business. In this way no one person is obtrusively singled out as the senior member of the team. As a note: The second in command is seated on the left—not the right—in Japan.

Many of the better meeting rooms in Japan have chairs that virtually "swallow" you. They are very, very deep, plush and comfortable. Too much so for people suffering from jetlag and who will, inevitably, experience a dozy feeling between 2 and 4 pm. To make matters worse for those being consciously challenged, there is a habit of turning all the lights off during projector presentations. There is nothing wrong with asking that the lights be kept on, or that only the front row of lights nearest the screen be dimmed. Better to ask this than having to re-direct your focus from the presentation to staying awake.

If you find it unbearably hot, try to make it through about the first fifteen minutes or so with your jacket on. At this point it is acceptable to ask to remove it. The Japanese team you are meeting will seem nearly impervious to the heat and may not offer to take your coat. Again, better to ask if you can take it off than having a Mississippian stream of sweat roll down your back and brow for two hours. There is nothing wrong with inquiring at the outset of the meeting if it would acceptable to strip off your suit coat, but, personally, I prefer to first settle in and establish the business mood. With the Japanese being respecters of form and substance, this might be better accomplished by remaining in a formal mode from the outset and then getting a bit more casual as you go.

The Meeting

So you're all settled into the big leather sofa seats and you're ready to kick-off the meeting. Inevitably, you will begin by giving a short self-introduction—again. There is a tendency to repeat this function in the larger context of all the participants. In a way, this is a good thing. During the blitzkrieg of business cards that assailed you as you entered the room, you probably had little chance to match a name with a face. By having a second round of introductions once everyone is seated allows you to do a couple of very useful things: First, you can lay out the business cards in front of you to correspond to where their owners are seated with respect to yourself. This makes it easier to call people by their names later on as your head begins to be filled with other data. Second, it allows you to sort out the slew of "managers" and more accurately identify who the key players are *vis-à-vis* where they are sitting.

Separating the wheat from the chaff can be especially difficult. The hierarchy of the Japanese company lends itself to having a flock of people with the titles "General Manager" or "Manager" making it virtually impossible to sense who is above whom in the pecking order. To be able to make this discrimination from the onset is crucial since there can be a very large disparity between a General Manager on the lower end of the spectrum and one on the upper end of the spectrum. Seating-wise, the man in charge will almost always be seated in the center of the table, as it is situated lengthwise. On occasion a high-level proxy will sit here, but this is only in the case where the senior member arrives late or needs to leave early. Do not worry about the spread of cards that lies before you, it is neither unseemly nor rude. Many of the Japanese will be doing likewise.

With this second introduction out of the way, you move on to the agenda. If this is merely a meet-and-greet, the guest generally goes first. If you're beyond that stage, an agenda should be set prior to the meeting. Whether this has been provided by you—something I whole heartedly suggest—or by the company you are visiting, you can be sure that no matter how concretely you've agreed on the version *du jour*, there will be another confirmatory process prior to jumping into business. Again, this may not be a bad thing; especially, if you are in some very complicated negotiations or are addressing some particularly sensitive issues. Once you have verbally confirmed an agenda in the actual meeting room, it becomes a kind of "stick" that you can use to keep focused and on track should they wish to gloss over or skip sections, or find themselves on a tangent. Re-confirming an agenda can be a bit redundant, though, and you will need to develop a unique kind of patience at times to get through the ritual of form and format. Be prepared for last minute changes to the agenda as well. Oftentimes, the Japanese company will have had a meeting the day prior to your arrival to brief a senior member of the organization on what you are planning to discuss. This may not be the case for a first visit, but for any subsequent visit where the discussions become more pointed and less exploratory, this type of agenda refinement is pretty much standard. Most times, changes to the agenda are not consequential; westerners are able to roll with most punches. Unless you have developed a strategy that relies on the agenda as pre-agreed, any last-minute changes by your Japanese hosts may help you to identify what issues are most critical to them and can serve to give you an indication of where the largest stumbling blocks to a successful deal may lay.

The order of presentations varies. There are pros and cons to going first and for going last. In my experience, I have found that the Japanese like to present first during negotiations. There are a number of reasons for this. It allows them to get it out of the way quickly. The Japanese culture is not conducive to producing good presenters or good presentations. Making a presentation is a time consuming, brain racking process. It is not so much that you "make" a presentation as you "create" a presentation. Without any creative thread, attempts to coalesce ideas into a good presentation result in a laundry list of loosely connected thoughts, which, if studied for a time, may or may not convey a message.

Perhaps one of the most effective presenters in the western world was Steve Jobs. Watching him is like watching art in motion. Charismatic delivery coupled with well-illustrated slides provide for a smooth, comprehensive, easily understood transfer of information. In the end, he successfully drives his point home and manages to make an impression on the listener and the listener's memory. Simply, it has "snap-bang."

A typical Japanese presentation, on the other hand, seems robotic. Slides can consist of block text on white background. There will be little in the way of diversity. Slide titles do not always accurately reflect the slide contents and if one topic spills over into two or more slides, they are only differentiated by a simple numerical label; *e.g.*, "Pharmaceutical Pipeline (1); Pharmaceutical Pipeline (2); Pharmaceutical Pipeline (3); etc. Your Japanese presenter will most likely read directly from the slide with the distracting habit of using a laser pointer as a "bouncing ball."

Rarely will the presenter offer any new insights into the slides unless he is queried. Even then, you may not be able to get the answer for which you are looking. It also may have broken the presenter's stride and he may have a tough time getting back into the presenter groove again.

In the west we build our case by using logic that flows from theory through proofs to a conclusion and, if those are logical and reasonable, our argument will move the audience to our position. The Japanese have a different approach to persuasive presentations. They begin with the conclusion and follow that up with their rationale. In this sense, patience is needed to understand the "whys' and the "wherefores." Sit and listen and resist the urge to poke holes through the presentation on slide 2. It is likely that your questions will be answered in the slides that follow. When a Japanese presenter is inundated by a barrage of questions on his opening slides, he becomes confused and even more inarticulate. By jumping the gun—that is, not waiting for him to run his course—you are asking him to abandon his slide presentation as it is organized and makes sense to him, and instead to embark on an impromptu discourse. This is something that he is not going to be able to do well in Japanese much less in the English language. As a result, he will feel disadvantaged and then defensive.

To better understand the reasons behind the decision, perhaps a good technique would be to diligently sit through the explanation and then ask for a break. During this time, you can review the slides in an order you feel more comfortable, and then decide the validity of the argument. You may also be able to leverage some insight out of the other Japanese participants through an informal dialogue during the break. As one last check, I would go ahead and summarize the rationale in terms that you understand and bounce this off the presenter. Keep in mind that he is now going through the same process from which you've emerged; that is, looking at the argument from a perspective in reverse.

There is always a point—even in the west—where we have no more to say and find that it is time to wrap things up. It may be, too, that either you or the company you are visiting may be under some time constraints. More likely—and a common mistake—it is you, the visitor, who has too ambitiously scheduled your time in Japan and find yourself behind schedule. Better to let the Japanese know from the very start about when is your dead stop. The best thing, though, is not to schedule more than one meeting per half day if you are in Tokyo. Start as soon as you can in the morning. Typically 10 am is appropriate. Likewise, in the afternoon Japanese companies get rolling at around 1 pm; however, I recommend giving the stragglers time to get back to their desks from lunch. Kicking off at 2 pm is a bit easier. One note: afternoons are much more flexible than mornings for Japanese. This is in part due the seemingly endless workday. They think nothing of inviting guests to begin a meeting a 4 pm given that their internal meetings can be slated to begin as late as 6 or 7 in the evening. Realizing that practicality, mostly in how much time it costs in Japan in terms of money and personnel exclusivities, generally dictates the ultimate time constraints, be wary that your commitments do not run counterproductive to your goals.

Almost always a deep well of silence will presage the end of the meeting. If you are finished, it is completely acceptable to take the bull by the horns and end the meeting. Being an overtly polite society, closings are perfused with an abundance of "thank yous." Handshakes and bowing ensue as you make your way to the door. In some of the better organizations, someone will accompany you to the front door. Some will take you even as far as the street and assist in hailing you a cab. It may be easy to misinterpret these courtesies, and walk away with an inflated idea of on what kind of note the meeting ended. It's just manners. You will find that even strangers on the street feel some responsibility towards you if you stop to ask them something.

Just as in any other situation, jotting down a quick

thank you note for the meeting goes a long way in establishing and maintaining a relationship. There are some Japanese that aren't diligent about this kind of communication, but you will find that others are. Keep in mind that form, process, procedure, and people are the driving elements from which impressions and, ultimately, decisions stem.

Two things to keep in the front of your mind at all times during a meeting; these two you will always encounter. First is something called "*aizuchi*." This is the practice of Japanese listener frequently nodding his head or voicing hums or grunts, particularly when the dialogue is directed towards him. Westerners have a tendency to interpret this as agreement. This is not necessarily so. In fact, it more likely means that your sound waves are reaching his ears, and he is acknowledging that he hears you. It is a form of respect to the speaker. You may note that the higher on the corporate hierarchy the listener occupies, the less you will encounter this custom.

The second thing to always remember is that, in English, the Japanese say what they can—not necessarily what they want to. Anyone who has had to use a foreign language for communication readily understands this. You are limited by what you know and to what customs you have been exposed. With those limitations, you speak and act without certainty that those words or actions are appropriate to the situation and that they accurately convey ideas in the same manner as if said or done by a native.

There is another danger in listening: People—westerners and Asians alike—tend to judge people on their articulation in speak. The better the sentence constructs, the better the vocabulary; the more intelligent the person. Never forget that, despite a simple or limited speech pattern, the Japanese are very, very bright people. Resist the urge to label them as less so when you hear their English.

What Happens Next

So the meeting went well, or at least you think so. Let's assume for the moment that there was some perceived interest. Let's see what happens next internally on the Japanese side.

First, there will be minutes written. Someone will be designated to write up the minutes of the meeting in Japanese. If there wasn't a native English speaker present, you are relying solely on the ability of a Japanese native to correctly interpret what transpired at the meeting as it relates to the business you conducted in English. This is predicated on two awfully big assumptions: First, that the person drafting the minutes is functional in both English and Japanese; and second, that the same person is also proficient in international business. Neither of these is a foregone conclusion. In fact, under normal conditions for a mid-sized Japanese company, I would be surprised if the individual met either of these criteria much less both.

It can be frustrating to discover that the Japanese minutes submitted to their senior management that you believe will help endorse your business proposition isn't an accurate account of the meeting. The "interpreter's" qualifications can range from having only junior/senior high school English topped off with some university classes to having studied "vigorously" on their own or to having spent time in an English-speaking country. Relying on their formal, compulsory education is frightening if you think of this in terms of how their US counterparts spend time in junior/senior high school learning languages. Comparatively speaking, US students that emerge from these language studies are much more versed at actual, practical communications than their Japanese equals. Grammatically, the US students may be inferior, but let's never forget the purpose of language is to be able to convey ideas and not necessarily to be technically proficient. The latter helps the former, but is not a prerequisite to a successful dialogue. The Japanese, by and large, spend their time parsing grammar. They can read and understand written English better than most foreign students of the language, but speaking and listening skills are still often quite poor.

Then there are the many and numerous nuances associated with English. Being a smattering of Celtic, Norse, Saxon German, Norman French and Latin, the dialects that abound in the US alone are myriad. Moving outward, there are differences between English in English speaking countries. Determining "standard" English can be controversial. One need only consider the long running lingual dispute between the US and Great Britain, or between the Brits and the Australians.

Even if a Japanese speaker could master an English dialect, there is no way that the speaker could absorb the finer points of the language, or get a native's instinctive and immediate understanding for phrases or accents that lie outside the spoken dialect. No amount of book studying can help. Even living abroad for 10 to 15 years tends to be insufficient. And keep in mind that the reverse is also true. If you trot out your Japanese 101—or graduate language skills for the matter—you cannot help but pale in comparison to the Japanese native. Lest we forget, language is a compilation of history and culture, and mastering that skill is lived rather than learned. Knowing this, keep the English simple, pointed, and polite during your meeting. Don't try to be impressive or pullout leftover SAT words thinking that you're making an impression on anyone. The fact that you can speak in consecutive complete sentences is impressive enough. Keeping it simple can aid in the Japanese businessman's understanding and, by extension, the ease a rapidity of you moving closer to sealing a deal.

The drafter's ability to put the events of the meeting into an international business context depends on what that individual's role is—and has been—in the company. It may also have a great deal to do with the industry with which you are associated. Banking, investment, and securities will provide a much more reliable common business foundation than will technical industries, such as pharmaceuticals and electronics. In the former, international business is the mainstay from the get-go, while in the latter it is more of an after thought. Companies whose core competencies are technical in nature do not always employ outsiders for their business functions. For technology related companies, they hire

105

staff with scientific or technical backgrounds and their business functions are largely subsidized from the excesses or rotations of that staff. As employees progress in years, they are soon put into one of three categories: technical career track; administration career track; or no career track. The first are the brilliant ones. There is no fear of them ever being mis- or re-assigned since the innovation and products the company needs to continue being profitable come from this class. The administrators are competent but not overly brilliant scientists that are pushed out of the technical hierarchy by the advent of newer blood coming in. In short, they are "cycled." The last group consists of the hiring "mistakes" that are pawned off to any internal group within the company that is willing to take them. Under the Japanese lifelong employment system, it is very difficult to dismiss these individuals once hired.

There is, unfortunately, a peppering of the "untouchables," or those that are deigned to be useless. These individuals find homes in the corporate hierarchy when management is hunting for people to fill its ranks. A request from a company's administrative section for personnel is looked upon by a good manager as an opportunity to cut dead wood. The unsuspecting group making a request finds out only much later that they were the means by which another group could clean house. Even in Japan, bad news travels fast. Once the transfer is completed, the options available to them are now severely limited. In a Japanese system, a transferee must be accepted by the group to which he wishes to transfer, and once a transferee is labeled as an ineffectual addition to a group, no other group in their right mind will take him, dooming the individual—and the group to which he has been relegated.

By and large, the business development group in tech companies seems to be where a lot of dead wood washes ashore. This bodes ill for those westerners who want to make inroads into establishing a business relation with a Japanese firm. Not only are these people not really technically proficient, but they lack the ability—at least by Japanese standards—to participate in Japanese business. Although labeled "Business Development" much of the domestic business is generated by sales and "new" business is generated by a top-driven policy. Many times, it is research driven and not revenue driven. The Business Development & Licensing (BD&L) unit is merely the worker ants acting upon the queen's orders. It's neither inventive nor difficult work.

And this is, to some degree, where much of your challenge lies. Especially from an international perspective. For some reason the Japanese make a distinction between standards for international business and those for domestic business. Almost like they are two wholly separate things. You are going to find that they will try things in the international arena that they would never, ever consider trying on a domestic scale. What this means is that not only is there a chance that are they not approaching international business as it is usual and customary, but they are not even abiding by their own national norms.

An ounce of prevention, as they say, is worth a pound of cure, and so anticipating these issues is paramount to

107

saving a slew of miscommunication and lots and lots of wasted time. Assuming that without some outside assistance internal communication at the Japanese company may not accurately represent what you thought transpired should encourage you to proactively work to correct—or better yet, head off—whatever misconceptions may be transmitted to decision-makers. Focus and prepare yourself against the myriad of things that can go wrong rather than taking a reactive posture. Absent communication to the contrary do not assume everything is in the affirmative. and is going according to plan. After all, it's not the good things that we need to prepare for—these are our expectations—but it's the unexpected things that throw the proverbial wrench in the works. With this philosophy in hand, succeeding is all that much more possible—and closer.

From their six years of emphasis on grammar, the Japanese tend to read English better than they can write, hear or speak the language. It would be, then, beneficial to write your own very brief but comprehensive minutes on the meeting and deliver them as soon as possible to your Japanese counterpart. Hours after the meeting would not be too soon. The stress here is on "brief" and "comprehensive." If you are too detailed or verbose, it will take time for your counterpart to digest what you sent, compare it to his notes, and prepare something for his management team.

If the meeting is one that promises to be opportunistic, part of the minutes may be a section for what the Japanese term "homework" (*shukudai*). These are action items on which either your team or theirs need to follow-up.

Whether it is additional information, compilation of data, the drafting of confidentiality agreements, or whatever; smart money sets deadlines for these activities before leaving the meeting. Without them, you will likely finish your tasks in a somewhat timely fashion, but need to wait for what seems like forever to get their replies. This is primarily for two reasons. First, you are operating in your native language making the supply of information mostly a simple a matter of formatting. Most of what you will need to supply is already in English and is probably lying around in one form or another. Consolidation and some editing are all that is usually required. Second, your approval and consent process for sending information outside your company probably boils down to a few individuals at the most.

Taking a look at the other side of the coin, your Japanese counterpart will likely need to sit down and really look at what he promised to deliver. Then he needs to find out where this information is located—or if they even have it. Then comes the translation of the information into English. Once this has been accomplished, the document needs to be staffed over a wide range of internal agencies all of which need to give their stamp of approval—sometimes literally. This rarely happens without no small amount of interdepartmental meetings, and revision upon revision upon revision of the original document. This all takes a great deal of time. Any promises of having follow-up information in your hands within one week of the meeting should be viewed with a great deal of skepticism. Depending on the kind and extent of information you may require, it is not unreasonable to allow them two weeks to get this done.

At this stage, expect and set reasonable, but laxed deadlines. Japanese operate off a "precedent" principle, and may view any changes in the duration it takes you to reply as a bad omen. Suddenly a perceived crisis will arise when, in fact, there is none. Something that may help avoid such situations is, rather than the more informal homework list, collectively draft an "Action Item" table after critical meetings. Designating who does what and by when, and having mutual agreement on it, is something tangible that can serve to assuage any false sense of panic on either side with respect to deliverables.

Translation takes the lion's share of the time and is, perhaps, the most underestimated in terms of effort and assets needed. The reason for this is that there has been traditionally a long-standing attitude towards English that runs deep in the Japanese psyche. They believe that changing from Japanese to English is along the same lines as throwing a light switch or plugging variables into an equation.

This "plug and chug" mentality remains a mystery to those of us living the moment. Could it be a result of their English studies being so academic? To some degree this makes sense. The Japanese practice grammar much as they practice mathematics. They repeat a particular mantra over and over and over again, replacing one small element in each iteration with something new. "I have a ball, I have a cat, I have a book, I have a *(ad nauseam)*. From this, a common misperception develops where English is a matter of set structures consisting of variables that can be mixed and matched.

Unfortunately, no language works this way and so what ends up happening is that either a single person is designated to translate the information, or it is out-sourced to a translation company. In the first case—and if they have no native speaking staff available—the document that ends up in your hands can read like cipher. Seemingly random words arrayed in halfway decent grammar. The result is that the communication becomes vague and more than one meaning can be gleaned from it.

If the company elects to use an outside translation service, what you get may be a bit better in quality. This depends on if the company took the time to look for a translation service that caters to their particular industry and if that service has competent native speakers on staff. Many of the translation companies found in Tokyo rely heavily on college students who are majoring in English. The fine-tuning is sometimes—but not always—performed by a native speaker.

The work coming out of these translation "sweatshops" varies in quality but no matter how good or bad, it still needs to be checked internally before the document leaves the company. This means that someone, be it a native speaker or a Japanese one, needs to compare the final product with the original Japanese text. And this does take some time. A lot of time. In the case of a Japanese reviewer, it may go a bit quicker but with more questionable results. When examining a document written for a professional audience and using an appropriate language level, a Japanese versed in the field may understand the vast majority of it. On the other hand, if the document is stylistically written using more business-like and less technical prose, the chances are that the Japanese reviewer will not be able to grasp the meaning of the entire document.

If a native speaker is on hand, and he is tasked with checking the document after it returns in-house from an outside translation service, he will probably take nearly as much time as the translation service. In effect, that person is repeating exactly what the service did absent the actual writing. No two people use the same style of writing and few people would translate the same Japanese text in the same way. This gives way to time spent amending text to fit more with personality rather than with being more accurate. The difference between the translation service and the in-house native speaker is that the latter works in, is responsible for, and is familiar with the English that leaves the Japanese company. The former is not.

Often times it is better to just task the translation to the in-house native speaker from the start. One problem lies in the fact that these employees very seldom have blocks of free time that they can dedicate solely to a large translation job. On the contrary, they are kept quite busy if the company is engaged in moderate international business. What this means to you is that the material you requested may need to pass through several hands with the strong possibility of work duplication. While this is frustrating, it is unavoidable and, in fact, you're not going to want the ten-cent version. You're going to want the three-week $1000 version. Anything short of that can be a very real source of inaccuracy and, in the end, you'll have to re-do the work at the expense of even more time.

Knowing that asking for specific information—especially something that's going to have to be generated by the Japanese company—can add significantly to the overall time it takes in the deal process, you should critically assess exactly what information is "must-have" at each phase of the deal and what is "nice-to-have." Nice to have things should be viewed as just that: Nice to have, but not necessary. If you ask for it, the Japanese will divert assets to supply it. Those assets may be better directed in other areas. In industries like pharmaceuticals, everything will eventually be needed in English, but you, as the western company bringing the asset in, ought better take the lead, and stage the translation work to enable your own development machine to keep moving forward. Whatever happens, don't be misled by promises of information delivery that sound too rosy. It plain and simple is not going to happen. If it does, chances are the work is not up to international standards and a large part of it will need to be overhauled.

If time, personnel, and budget permit, much of the "nice to know" items can be acquired during an in-person due diligence visit. The advent of on-line due diligence rooms has all but displaced—or at the very least minimized—this dated due diligence practice. Despite that, it is still generally a good idea to put boots on ground to verify data. It is a particular good venue to round up all the odds and ends that perhaps don't fit neatly into any one single diligence category. Supplying your potential Japanese partner a comprehensive list of what you'd like a week or two before the visit will all but guarantee everything you need will be waiting.

113

Inevitably, there will be some communication back and forth as you both explore the possibility of collaboration. One thing that can be confusing as you swap messages is what is progressing in real time. When the Japanese are sending their messages, you are tucked up safely in bed. As you read those messages, it is their turn to sleep. On a conscious level, I think we all understand this. On an operating level, we do not. We interpret what we see as an event that is happening right then and there, and expect the responses or actions be taken as if you were in New York and they were in Chicago. So, expressions along the lines of "by the close of business on Friday," or "you'll have it first thing tomorrow morning," need to be thought through from two different viewpoints: Yours and theirs. More often than not, your "close of business on Friday" works out to be "first thing Saturday morning" for the Japanese. Not a big deal if it's something you need by then, but if the Japanese need material by close of business on their Friday, you're looking at having to send it by the close of business on your Thursday. Best advice: Be flexible about receiving information; be prompt about sending information. Always try to be a bit early. Although you may have promised something by a certain date, you can be sure to receive e-mails a few days prior to that wondering when you will *actually* be sending the material.

While correspondences by e-mail can be a bit inconvenient in this respect, communicating by telephone or video requires lifestyle changes. Even though daylight savings time attenuates things somewhat, you are still almost a complete circadian cycle different, making a mutually agreeable time for any interactive meeting virtually impossible. Calling Japan to catch someone at their desk means that you could be dialing 7 pm (8 in summer) to reach them at 9 am, or 3 am (4 in summer) to connect with them by 5 pm. This does not even factor in the actual time you'll need to spend on the phone to complete your business. This can take an hour or two in itself, and added to the time above, makes for a real hard schedule.

In actual practice, what seems to work well is an early evening call from the US east coast, and an early morning call from Japan. On standard time, a 6 pm (EST) call from the States puts you in touch with your Japanese counterparts at 8 am. In winter, you're looking at 7 pm to reach out and touch the Japanese at 8 am.

From Europe, it's just the opposite. A morning call from central Europe works best. Using standard time, there is an eight-hour difference, meaning that calling at 9 am (CET) reaches Japan at 5 pm. Again, summertime is a bit better as calling the same time has you talking with your Japanese colleague at 4 pm. Compare to the States, this is a much more relaxed situation and provides better for the lengthy conversations that tend to ensue.

Take comfort in knowing that Japanese do not really like to talk on the phone or converse through video media. At least in business and with foreigners. This stems largely from the language handicap. As any ex-foreign language student or foreign speakers can easily testify, when one communicates in another language, one relies heavily upon the body language of the speaker to understand fully what message is being transmitted. Likewise, the foreign speaker can quickly assess how much is understood by the foreign listener from the listener's body language. Especially when someone is totally lost.

Deprived of this and relying solely on the speaker's voice is terrifying for the Japanese. It should also be terrifying for you, but for different reasons. Generally, the main purpose of a phone call is to clarify the things that seem to have been muddled in written correspondences. An interactive venue tends to clear things up rather quickly as you can explain a bit more in-depth and can field specific questions from the receiver. That is, of course, assuming that you both can clearly understand each other.

In the States, we have, historically, relied heavily on the telephone to cut through the chase and speed up the process. E-mails and letters can be ignored but a person's voice commands attention. We tend to believe that this will be the case across the board, internationally speaking. This can be a very damaging misconception when dealing with the Japanese. In fact, when you are set on improving a situation with a phone call, you are probably muddying the waters even more. The basis for this is that your verbal, spoken English has a lesser chance of being absorbed and understood to the extent that you would like. In particular, if you are dealing with scientific types, there will be a great amount of apparent agreement without the accompanying understanding. The result: The Japanese will walk away even more confused. Suddenly, and unexpectedly, you will find yourself in a situation you would have never thought possible and it may exacerbate the situation you were trying to originally clarify. And it will take more time to clear this up—a face-to-face meeting will almost always be precipitate. Good advice here is to minimize using the telephone or video. If it has to be done, I would lean more towards video teleconferencing; particularly, the rise of Google Meet, Zoom, and other commercial conferencing computer applications makes this less complicated than in the past

If you decide to go the telephone or video teleconference route, or it becomes an inevitability, it is best to be proactive in following up. Just like your first encounter, waiting only gives the Japanese an opportunity to either think too deeply about what transpired or to come up with alternate realities. Keep it simple and short. Address only the issues that were discussed and be sure to focus on the clarifications for which the meeting was held. Bullet statements are generally pointed enough to where there exists only a small chance of being misconstrued.

The thing I try to keep in mind in all my communications with the Japanese is: Will the person understand what I am saying? You often need to adjust your style, vocabulary, grammar, and speaking speed depending on the listener. Again, coming off as too "intelligent" or too "articulate" will be counterproductive. Clear, simple, and efficient communication is, perhaps, the most difficult kind. Anyone can ramble. Choosing your words for clarity, using basic grammar, and keeping speech short and structured is a skill that will make your life negotiating with the Japanese much easier—and quicker.

Activities Leading to a Draft Agreement

If the communication has gone well to this point and if you are focusing on building a relationship with the Japanese company with which you want to do business, you probably will shortly arrive at the juncture where a secrecy agreement becomes necessary. Both Westerners and the Japanese have oscillated on how they approach secrecy agreements over the last couple of decades. In the distant past, westerners were quick to execute these types of agreements while the Japanese were hesitant. Then the opposite was true. Now, we are in a period where everyone is a bit reluctant to exchange confidential information unless there is some indication of real interest. What the future brings is anyone's guess.

Two-way secrecy agreements are very rare from the outset. Confidential obligations are normally laid on the licensee and not the licensor. Depending which side of the coin you are on, you need to be very careful of the information you give away. If the secrecy obligation falls squarely on your shoulders, the Japanese company will dole out only the information they think you'll need and not necessarily the information you want. I this respect, there are "levels" of secrecy. Found on one of the higher tiers is intellectual property. If you are the licensee, the Japanese will expect periodic reports as your evaluation progresses, and a final report indicating a "GO" or "NO GO" decision.

The terms "Confidentiality Disclosure Agreement" (CDA) and "Secrecy Agreement" (SA) are terms that are used interchangeably. Some firms prefer the former; some the latter. Some use them at random. For our purposes, I will use "CDA."

Naturally, everybody everywhere wants to use his own draft as the basis for the CDA; it makes the process much easier for that party. An unwritten rule, more of a custom really, is that the possessor of the confidential information supplies the first draft. When it comes right down to it though, CDAs are pretty much standard. It's pretty easy to see the parallels between one version and another. Easy, that is, if you are functional in English, have your own legal staff, and have a library of experience with them. Depending on the size of the company with whom you are interfacing, it can take days to pore through a five-page document.

Therefore, while it may not be customary, it is prudent for the sake of time to allow the Japanese to provide the first draft of a CDA no matter which way the information is flowing. At least take a look at it. This just helps speeds things along. The language is familiar to the Japanese reviewers and any changes you may have will be readily

119

observable. This decreases—enormously—the turnaround time between versions. Realistically, you can hope to have an executed copy of a CDA in hand anywhere between two to six weeks, depending on how "standard" is their first draft.

Now, compare this to what needs to be done if you supply the first draft. Once sent to the Japanese company, the business development team will need to dissect the document, almost line by line, word for word. They will need to compare your version to their own, confirming that all elements of theirs is included in yours. A time-consuming process to say the least. Once done, the document moves to the legal section for their comments.

This would be a good time to briefly explain the legal situation in Japan. Until very recently, becoming a lawyer in Japan was like becoming a member of the Augusta National Golf Club. Once you had the appropriate credentials, you needed years before being admitted having to suffer through a vicious cycle of application and rejection, application and rejection, application and rejection, until finally being granted admission. This, in part, stems from the test-taking culture of the Japanese in general. Lawyers are, perhaps, the best test-takers in the country. On par with doctors, they occupy one of the highest social strata in Japan. The joke is that they are one tier below God. Not totally an exaggeration. Very few people challenge or questions what comes out of a lawyer's office.

In fact, the bar to the bar is so high that many Japanese graduates of law schools do not even attempt the written and oral testing process, but, rather, join the legal staff of large companies. Once on the rolls, many companies will ship them off to the US to take the bar in one of the states. New York State is a popular choice since an accredited law school degree is not a pre-requisite to becoming a lawyer. After passing the bar in the US, they return to their company and embark on a career as a "pseudo" lawyer; that is, one who has the credentials but not the title of a Japanese lawyer.

Litigation in Japan is very low making the time a lawyer spends in court is very small. So much so that, at least for contract law, a legal staffer at a company may actually have more real-world experience than a certified Japanese lawyer. Many lawsuits are settled before coming to trial. The courts encourage these types of settlements and the lawyers do what they can to make this happen. The motivation for them not to go to court stems from the fact that a lawyer who "loses" a case finds future clients hard to find.

The important thing to remember here is that you are not dealing with officially legally qualified people when you do any contract work with a Japanese company. This can be to a great advantage, if the correct approach is made. For example, arguments for using Japanese law as the governing law can be quashed if the Japanese legal staff working on your agreement is certified to practice law in a US state but not Japan.

Without having actual lawyers review the agreements—and the same Japanese legal staff will review and comment on all the agreements—can put a trump card in your hand should the discussions come down to what is appropriate and proper. By simply asking what the

Japanese company's legal counsel recommends, and pushing the point of *actual* and *qualified* legal counsel, you can dismiss as unqualified whatever changes the in-house legal staff made.

For all agreements, the Japanese have a time-consuming review process called "*ukagaisho.*" It consists of a round robin approval of all the heads of the major groups involved in the business project. For each agreement, allow for about two weeks to clear this process. If the business development types you are interfacing with are good, they will have already smoothed this path and this then becomes a rubber stamp exercise. On the other hand, if he has done nothing to assist his senior managers' review of the documents, it can take quite some time to clear. He will have to go each manager from whom he needs approval and offer an in-depth explanation of what has been done, what steps are next, and what eventually he—the manager—needs to provide to support the deal. Also bear in mind that the longer the document, the longer this process may take.

Let's assume for the time being that you are the one receiving the confidential information. In my experience, more frustration lies with confidentiality obligations in this direction than *vice versa*. Let's also say you're satisfied with what you see and want to "test drive" the product. For my familiarity's sake, I'm going to use an example of a pharmaceutical development compound, but the procedure remains virtually identical no matter what product you are pursuing or what business you are in.

In order to get your hands on a sample, you will need to execute another agreement called a Material Transfer

Agreement (MTA). The time it takes to wade through this is considerably longer than a simple CDA. It is here that you will start to feel frustration set in. Depending on how the product is viewed and what strategic importance the Japanese place on it, you are liable to met with a great number of conditions that just do not fit with your way of doing business.

What you want to do with the product and *how* you want to evaluate it will come under close scrutiny. You will have to provide a summary protocol for the tests you plan to perform, and these will need to be "approved" by the Japanese company providing the product. From these protocols, an appropriate amount or number of the product will be determined and sent to you.

Certain evaluations will not be permitted. In the case of pharmaceuticals, neither chemical nor structural analysis will be allowed. Patents are niggardly disclosed at this point. Although they are, for the most part, open-source information, the paranoia of Japan prevents them from letting this information out of the company. The rationale is that you, as a potential competitor, would be able to read the patent, identify the loopholes, and develop a similar and superior product at a much faster pace than the Japanese. You would then be able to destroy—or at least damage—the company.

Should the Japanese agree to disclose published patents, there will be language in the agreement that will restrict what you can do with that public knowledge. It really can be handicapping if your company is active in that area. On the other hand, it is important to protect whatever intellectual property (IP) your firm develops and the fewer

123

people that know the details of your technology, the better. But as most people who deal with patents on a daily basis can attest, knowing the patent number may not equate to knowing the specifics of the technology. In the pharmaceutical industry, one patent may contain hundreds of variants of a basic chemical structure of which only a handful of compounds will actually work. Knowing the patent number in this case is not all that useful other than allowing the potential licensee get a good idea of patentability and freedom to operate.

Because you are actually about to handle the product, there may appear in the MTA restrictions on what you can do with respect to the technology being evaluated. Again, going back to our pharmaceutical example, do not be overly surprised if the Japanese ask that you do not file any patents that relate to the compound or its mechanism for a period of years. I have seen proposals that range from three to seven years. Other conditions may state that if you do generate IP related to the evaluated product, you must grant a fully paid, non-exclusive, worldwide, sub-licensable license to the Japanese company.

Agreeing to such proposals can effectually shut you down for a number of years. Depending on how badly you want to pursue the opportunity, you can either agree to the terms knowing that most small to mid-sized Japanese companies do not have the resources to follow all patents filed in any area, or you can pare down the language. You can usually get away with promising the grant of rights to only those claims of a patent that directly apply to the product being evaluated.

If you do encounter such a company, take solace in

knowing that all the other bidders are experiencing the same thing. But if the opportunity is a hot one, it will be the company that seamlessly overcomes this obstacle that will be perceived by the Japanese as the front-runner.

Non-disclosure of certain items can be rate limiting in your evaluation. I think most westerners accept this, knowing that the essential information will become available as the project moves forward. But this assumption goes hand-in-hand with the understanding that no decision will be required of them until they are in possession of all the relevant data. But this may not fit in with your Japanese counterpart's ideas.

To the Japanese, it is all about "level of interest." You will be constantly plagued by the question, "Can you tell us your level of interest?" The valve that releases the floodwaters of information is commitment. But it is difficult to provide very concrete feedback to this question without having all your questions answered. Any response you give is unavoidably qualified. "We're interested BUT…" The Japanese will not take this as a positive reply, focusing more on the "BUT" part rather than, "Yes, we have interest." It is difficult to convince the senior management at mid-level Japanese companies that a high level of interest and a need for additional information mutually co-exist.

For most Japanese companies, the turning point in the discussions lies with the performance of an official due diligence. There is a gulf between the connotation westerners have for the term "due diligence" and the one held by the majority of Japanese businessmen. To us, it is a long process that begins with first contact and ends with the signing of the agreement. The process is basically a cover-your-ass process undertaken to ensure that you're getting what you think you're getting and that the rights to whatever you're getting are free and clear. We need this to assure our own senior management that the opportunity is worth what we are paying and that the returns fall within our expectations. In the past—and to some extent even now—the Japanese due diligence is relegated to the part of the process where you take an investigational team to the company's facilities and delve into every nook and cranny to ferret out the weak links in the chain. In more recent times and with more progressive companies, the virtual due diligence room takes this place and how frequently you're in it gives them an indication of your interest. If, for some reason or another, your team hasn't logged onto the site for a period of time, the Japanese will begin to get unsettled, and even your missives explaining why will be met with skepticism and worry.

Your official due diligence signals to the Japanese your firm commitment. With mid-sized companies it is often still necessary to send a team to Japan on your own dime to review all the pertinent data. During your review, they will make everything available to you. If you can't find it, they will hunt it down for you. For the most part, no Japanese company will intentionally mislead you or try to bury any data or any results that are less than spectacular. On the other hand, due diligence is one of the greatest sources of miscommunications in the business development process. The major reason for this is that the questions that need to be asked are very specific and technical in nature. This makes a complete understanding by the Japanese very difficult. Additionally, the individuals who are keepers of the information or who are the actual producers of the data may have very, very limited language abilities. This results in taking many, many a wrong path. To get back on track takes realignment of thinking and, in many cases, the resetting of the situation.

Some diligences need to take place over multiple sites. Travel between locations can take a big bite out of available time. If all the sites are not all located on the main island of Honshu, it may take close to a day to get there. There is nothing wrong or unseemly with putting the hubris on the Japanese to get all the documentation to one central location. You are traveling halfway around the world. It is reasonable to demand that they accommodate a single location. If the diligence extends to site inspections, you may prefer to inspect that site's documents in their native habitat.

Time. Time is a commodity that Japanese do not treat with the same volatility as we. Determining how long you should spend on an official diligence is difficult. Try to keep it less than four days, if possible. A small- to medium-sized company will be dedicating the lion's share of its resources to support your visit and it is a bit unreasonable to keep everyone tied up for more than a week. On the other hand, don't shortchange yourself with time. As the adage goes, "It's better to have it and not need it than need it and not have it." You can always go home early. It's difficult to rearrange everyone's schedule at the last minute to extend a visit.

Despite your jetlag, the Japanese will think nothing of working well past the witching hour and onto the dawn.

To them, overtime is not in their vocabulary and is a non-issue. Gauge this as you proceed. At some point there will be a law of diminishing returns. There is no problem with you shutting down for the day. If you do, try to stop at a convenient place in the agenda.

The order of inspection items should be left up to the Japanese company unless you bring team members who need to arrive late or leave early. It should be sufficient to provide them with a list of questions and items to be reviewed. Most Japanese companies can build an agenda out of this. There will be additions to that list, however. Typically, the first half-day will be spent by your host giving an overview of the company, its capabilities and highlighting the progress and merits of the opportunity you are there to assess. Lunches are a bit fluid and can range from a light repast of finger sandwiches to a full course at an elegant restaurant. Being from the west, it may help speed up the entire process if you suggest keeping lunch as a light, working meal.

Some companies may ask you to execute a separate CDA prior to your diligence visit. This will be more focused on intellectual property—patent items, proprietary information, and know-how. Most, if not all, of these are likely covered by the initial CDA, but despite your objections you may be faced with this situation anyway. If you are asked to execute another CDA, this should heighten your perceptions that this Japanese company is exhibiting a more than average penchant for paranoia. Adjust your strategy accordingly. If the deal is something in which you are truly interested, make an extra effort to reassure the Japanese of the mutual prosperity of the deal

128

and emphasize their crucial role in making it a success.

To publish, prosecute, and maintain patents takes a serious amount of cash—something that is in short supply at small to mid-sized companies. Consequently, there may be a preponderance of know-how and proprietary information which, if not diligently safeguarded could be the basis for patents by some other, larger company who is better funded.

The conduct of an official due diligence will, as with every meeting, produce a list of items on which you either have further questions or that were not answered for whatever reason. This should be part of your out-brief and written down somewhere so that everyone can look, see, add, or subtract, as appropriate. I prefer the use of a white board that can print. Once you get back to your hotel for the evening and before that final nightcap, send an e-mail to your counterpart with the very same summary that was on the white board along with the deadlines agreed upon for their resolution.

A brief note on white boards. These are great tools and one of your best friends when dealing with the Japanese. As we have mentioned, English as a written language is much easier for them to understand than English as a spoken language. With the Japanese being a high-context culture—in particular, their written language consists of ideograms (kind of pictures) and not characters representing phonics—visualization is one of the quickest ways to comprehension. This idea is best carried over int your slide presentations as well.

Once you've made your report to them on your due diligence results, and they have satisfactorily replied, it would be a good idea to suggest a term sheet. One problem you may encounter is that the smaller Japanese companies seldom know the real market value of what they have. They almost always are drawing from a very limited—and often outdated—list of prior experiences; almost none of them reflect the leading valuation methods being used at the time.

And deep down they know that they can't do this. So rather risk sounding foolish by asking too little or too much—especially in the financials—invariably their term sheet draft will arrive with only the most general items filled in. Be prepared to walk them through the generalities of your proposals always remember the "saving face" rules.

Along the way, and depending on in what business you are engaged, there may be a necessity for scientific meetings. These tend to take place after the release of critical path data, upon the completion of your evaluation, or when you need to inspect their research, development, and/or manufacturing facilities to satisfy either an internal criterion or a regulatory one. They often run a separate, albeit loosely related, course to business activities. These scientific meetings resemble professional football games: You bring a large contingent of your biggest hitters from your science groups, and they bring together all the science guys they can muster related to the project, and then you both square off with one another. If the meeting is held on their home turf, things may get a bit out of hand. The venue will be jam packed with anyone remotely associated with the project. This can be down to the guy who calibrated such-and-such a device for a test conducted ten years ago. While it's great to have such a wealth of human knowledge in one place at one time, it isn't always conducive to running a smooth meeting. The pace will be incredibly slow as virtually every question you have is filtered down to the lowest level—and then back up the chain.

Be on the lookout for the "translators," if any. These are more than likely people taken from their own assets—either from the business development side or the technical departments. These people may or may not have an idea of what is going on; they may have been tasked just for this As a result, they may not speak the requisite argot and you may have to play a guessing game to fully understand what they are describing. Even in the Japanese language they may not have a good grasp as to what their own people are trying to convey.

Obviously, this can be frustrating. The key to circumventing this is to have, as much as possible, all the technical questions written down in advance or items you plan to discuss. If the Japanese company does end up bringing translators who are not skilled in the area, at least they will have some forewarning as to the vocabulary that will arise and can have their own technical staff coach them how and what to answer.

But in order to accomplish this, though, first you have to be suspect that the participants in your scientific meeting will not all be scientists or technical sorts. The only way to possibly know this is to exchange a list of the names of all the attendees beforehand as soon as the topics of discussion have been identified. If their list includes people with strange job titles with respect to the meeting at hand, you can be pretty sure that these are going to be the translators. Confirm their roles immediately. This may help you in knowing what appropriate language and descriptions to use when drafting questions or presentations. It won't be practical to use layman's English in everything—by nature, the subjects you broach will be complicated and have specific techno-ese associated with them. What you can do, though, is draft written material so that the sentence structure and supporting vocabulary make the technical words standout. Most Japanese tech-types should recognize English words that relate to their industry especially if they are keeping up with the trades and other professional news sources.

Be prepared for long, hard days for scientific meetings. It seems that no matter what kind of compensatory factor you use, you're always behind. Without sounding like a broken record, the key to turning a four-day visit into a two-day one is knowing exactly what you're looking for and preparing the Japanese for that adequately in advance. After you begin your meeting, resist the urge to get sidetracked. You will inevitably find that one door opens to two that opens to four and so on *ad nauseam*. If necessary, spend some time on an earlier visit to lay the groundwork. A cursory inspection, or "tour," of a facility you've earmarked for an inspection can save a great deal of time later on. You can take that impression home with you and begin to focus on particular areas of interest. Addressing these first and then moving to more routine checks may be a better use of your time. In this way, if you suddenly find yourself out of time, at least you covered the potential showstoppers.

132

One good thing about the Japanese when it comes to due diligence or inspections is that they do prepare well. They will haul virtually every document relating to the project and cram it all into a room along with the corresponding personnel responsible for each document. Anything you want to see should be at your fingertips. One caveat, however: The Japanese are not particularly insightful or creative, meaning that this excellent preparation will be based on your "wish" list of items to check. If you wander outside this box, you may very well experience some difficulties in getting what you ask for in a timely manner. They will break a leg trying, but the system moves slower than what you may be used to and it may take some time.

Until now, we've been operating under the assumption that you will be the one in-licensing. It may very well be that it is the other way around: you are the one providing goods or services. The agreements you need—or want—to satisfy you company's requirements may differ from a Japanese company. In general, you have the upper hand when dealing out, and stand a better chance of sidestepping some of the bureaucratic processes one would need to go through if roles were reversed.

The Japanese are very competitive oriented, but they are not very perceptive. I don't mean it to sound like they are obtuse, but the vastly different approaches to business have them looking right sometimes when they should really be looking left. If you do not tell them directly that they are in a competitive situation, they may not ask and, by not asking, assume—or pretend to assume—that they are the sole company vying for this opportunity. Later, when they discover that there were other bidders, they feel betrayed and appalled. Make sure they know from the outset—or as soon as is practicable—that they are in a competitive environment. You will find that they reply a bit faster and are a bit more accommodating. It can sometimes be difficult to keep them competitive, though. If you find that they are merely matching the terms and conditions of the other bidders and you want them to remain relevant in the process, you may have to "coach" them; that is, place a seed in their mind that, to win the hand, they have to more than "see" the other payers. They have to raise.

The language barrier is often to blame here. As Americans—and by extension—westerners, we do not condone out-and-out lying during business discussions. It's bad for a couple of reasons: First, you tend to burn bridges that you may want later; second, you can go to jail. And so instead of tempting the Fates, we choose to check our banter and speak the truth in a roundabout fashion. Through omissions. It's not just what I say that's important, but what I *don't* say. For a culture that avoids directness in almost all things, it is surprising that the Japanese do not pick up on this. Perhaps it lies with the reputation that westerners have for being brutally direct. Whatever the reason, they sometimes do not often realize that there are layers to conversations that taken one-by-one are misleading, but taken as a whole accurately describe the situation.

To avoid bad blood later on, it is important to be as straightforward with a Japanese contender as you can without compromising your strategy. One cannot

134

automatically assume by talking with them that they fully grasp the circumstances surrounding them. As an illustration, colleagues of mine—and they were rather highly placed in the organization—pursued an in-licensing opportunity without my assistance. Everything from the correspondences to the face-to-face meetings was done completely by this self-designated task force. They made numerous visits to the American company, some unsolicited. I found out only later that the American company was being tight lipped about the opportunity, and was reluctant to proceed at the pace the Japanese had set. They did allow a due diligence visit that confirmed the value of the deal. In a bid to put off the Japanese, the American company raised its asking price by 50% on the grounds that no deficiencies were found in the due diligence. Still the Japanese were not discouraged and, despite this being a tidy sum to be paid from the company coffers, pushed a first draft of an agreement. Two weeks later a press release was found in the pages of an industry trade magazine that the company had out-licensed to another company.

When I talked to one of the delegates from our company, and heard about the visits they were making and looked at some of the correspondences, it took little time to understand that these guys were not where they thought they were. Instead, they were being fed delaying tactics and, from my impression, were being used as a stalking horse to jack up the price of the deal. The American company played this against their preferred partner and eventually sealed the deal with them. The Japanese screamed "Foul" and went so far as to investigate litigation. Naturally, no lawyer—Japanese or American—wanted to touch this case.

Something that has remained unsaid until now, but is of great significance, is that the Japanese may employ an international lawyer to assist them in these deals. They will not hide this from you, but, on the contrary, want to make you very aware of the fact. This is tantamount to saying "No tricks, now. I've got an international lawyer who knows what's going on." Well, yes and no. First, it's not such a big deal to us. We all have lawyers. But remember, to the Japanese, having a lawyer is like having a hotline to God. Since there has been no long-term relation with the Japanese, the law firms the Japanese typically find are like guns for hire. Most mid-sized Japanese companies do not conduct international business as a matter of routine so they do not see the need to keep a law firm on a retainer. This tends to distant the law firm from its Japanese client. They simply do not have a horse in the race other than their fees, and they approach the deal accordingly.

Consequently, the lawyers the Japanese tend to retain are imbued with a "Go to the motor pool" mentality, as we used to say in the Army. Particularly dense privates who are in the military for just a paycheck, will do exact what they are told. There will be no exercise of creativity or a deductive thinking process. So, when you tell a private to go to the motor pool, he does just that. He goes there and sits down and waits. You didn't tell him to perform any duties or see his NCO for instructions, although that was what you implied. Even if he is confronted by another officer or NCO, and they ask him what he is supposed to be doing, he will confidently reply that he was told to come to the motor pool by Lieutenant so-and-so. To the passing authoritarian, this is a sufficient answer and they proceed on their merry way leaving the private in the same state of idleness as when they found him.

This is just what the lawyers for hire are doing. Japanese companies, being secretive by nature, do not always let the lawyers in on what goals are being sought, what limitations exist, and what latitude the lawyers have in negotiations. This is frustrating to the legal firm but not enough to decline the client—or the fee. After all, win, lose, or draw, lawyers always get paid. So, they do exactly what they are told and not a bit more.

Now how much special effort you want to exert to ensure that your Japanese bidders are on par with other bidders, is up to you. Be aware, though, that small to mid-sized companies do not operate on a "business is business" level. They tend to hold grudges, and never forget or forgive a slight. On the other hand, their institutional memory is rather short and leadership tends to cycle roughly about every three years, so in the long term, the ill-will harbored is of no great lasting consequence. In the west, larger organizations can be suing each other on one front and negotiating a new business arrangement on another. In the pharmaceutical industry this is often the case. Companies do not view negative interactions as being personal affronts, but merely as exercising strategic options.

Again, the fulcrum in the process is due diligence. Once past this point, the Japanese feel that they have expressed their solid interest and should be considered as a final candidate. Consequently, they rush to perform this task. It is often the premise in Japanese business of first come, first serve. This is especially true from a small- to mid-sized company perspective where they are ecstatic at having even one prospect. This thought process somehow carries over into their world view and is manifest in the belief that if they are the first to a deal milestone—again, almost always due diligence is taken as the critical marker—then they deserve some special considerations. These considerations are to be of a magnitude to offset their size or inexperience and to put them more on par with larger, more established competitors.

People and process. These describe how the Japanese approach opportunities. Expediting a process should give one a reputation of a mover and shaker. Establishing and maintaining personal relationship should establish one as a partner of choice. Now, we all know that having these qualities certainly helps in candidate selection; however, westerners are bottom line people. What can you do for me? How can you maximize benefits to me? Answers to these questions determine who moves to the winner's circle and who goes home with the booby prize. With a Japanese company, you will need to make them painfully aware of these from the first. They will still insist on including process and relations, and these never hurt. If you are seriously harboring the thought that a Japanese partner may be preferable, and would like to keep one or more Japanese firms in the mix, do not hesitate for one moment to figuratively yank them by the collar to get them back on track.

How to do this and still keep forward momentum? An occasional tactful scathing critique of a fluff presentation will serve the purpose just fine. This can be done quite simply. Just ask "Why." Fire a couple of those missiles home during a meeting and you will most likely find their presentation left in shambles. It is a bit humiliating so try not to over do it. To re-direct them back on the yellow brick road, offer them another chance to do the same presentation. If they are visiting you, you need not give any deadline. "Soon" is enough. On the other hand, if you are in Japan for the sole purpose of this presentation, giving them until the next day is fine. After all, you it's your dime and it never hurts to drive that point home. I think that you'll find that by doing this once or twice at the beginning, future presentations of the same caliber will be few and far between.

Some small- to mid-sized companies live under the belief that everyone in the world knows who they are and respects their reputations as businessmen. In truth, very few companies in the west have any idea of even the largest Japanese companies. Case in point: I worked for one of the largest chemical conglomerates in the Japan. As measured by sales, it ranks at or near number one. It perpetually resides in the top five ranked companies favored by university graduates. Yet, in the west, very few people recognize the name. If they do, they often mistakenly associated it with a product of another company of a similar name. If you want to impress the Japanese company with which you are dealing, learn a bit about them. Who they are. What they do. Products they have.

At the end of the day, it's important to be gracious in both winning and losing, no matter which side of the deal you are on. You never know when another opportunity may present itself, and you never can tell what position the contacts you have been working with will hold. Some may be the key decision-makers. Or even (in one case I had) the president. This makes maintaining corporate relations all that much more important.

No matter which side of the coin you find yourself on—in-licensing (buying) or out-licensing (selling), the process will remain the same but how you treat your counterpart does change. The strategic and competitive situation will, naturally, dictate how much you can push or pull. This seems obvious except for the fact that dealing with the Japanese can make this seems like throwing a baseball in outer space. With nothing to push against, both you and the ball will career apart in opposite directions with equal force. Japanese business is not grounded in the same ways in which westerners have become attuned. This makes any points of reference in deals either difficult to find or useless to interpret. By controlling the pace from the outset, by controlling the transfer of information, and by establishing a clear set of ground rules, the chances of a better overall experience and one that has greater chances of success can be greatly enhanced.

Contract Negotiations

Now comes the beginning of negotiations for a definitive agreement. This can be an exciting time or one filled with dread, depending on which partner you have selected and what experience you bring to the table. In many ways, it's like entering into marriage: You may think you know someone from the time you've spent together thus far, but it's only when you are in close proximity for an extended period of time do you really get an idea of all the quirks and idiosyncrasies—both good and bad—of the other person. You begin to see things as they truly are. Eyes heretofore blinded by pre-conceptions and dreamy hopes are suddenly opened. Sometimes rudely.

The Japanese do a good job keeping their innermost qualities—whatever they might be—hidden. If the path leading to these negotiations has been positive but frustrating, you've only glanced the tip of the iceberg. It, too, may have been fruitful and you may, indeed, have reaped what your expectations have sown. But it comes at a price. And just as with the selection process, good preparation and a solid, well thought out strategy can save many a sleepless night, or, at least, not a few raging headaches.

But for whatever reason, you've selected a Japanese company as a partner, or a Japanese company has selected you as theirs. Either way, it is never an easy thing to work cross-culturally and bring equal amounts of success to both parties. This is especially true when the gulf between the two cultures is as vast as that between the west and Japan. At the very beginning, I emphasized that there is a myriad of different ways to reach the same goal. This is the time to keep this mantra going deep inside your psyche because you may be sorely tested and this may be your only anchor in an otherwise turbulent time.

One inevitable frustration is what I call the triple standard. We all are familiar with those partners who push for things to their advantage in one respect but cry foul when turnaround is used as fair play. We work hard to mitigate this double standard and, oftentimes, the deal ends in tears. No one can stomach a long-term relation that is all take and no give. But it's our job as business development types to develop strategies to circumvent these double standards so that, in the end, we all get what we want. Or some of it anyway. Now enter the triple standard. This is something entirely different altogether, and it's like mentally moving from a squared power to a cubed one.

A triple standard is when two parties from two separate cultures are trying to do a deal and one party employs a tactic that would be a double standard in its own business environment but genuinely and honestly believes that standard is the usual and customary standard another. This is not maliciously done; it is done in earnest. Mostly it stems from a lack of exposure to the other culture and their way of doing business. For example, if a company under a given set of circumstances would only consider as a reasonable figure a royalty rate of, say, 15% if it were negotiating with its domestic peers, it proposes to you a figure of 65% because they think that this is how their partner normal approaches royalties.

To better understand when a triple standard is being used, we first must understand what is normal for a particular people in a similar situation. When it comes to the disparity between the west and Japan, there may seem to be little common ground for "normal." How would a Japanese company negotiate with another Japanese company? What proposals would be considered "normal" in that sense? What proposals would be considered strange or even teetering on the bizarre? It would be of great help for a western negotiator to know these things; however, there is little open-source material to help define these practices and, as we have already discussed, the Japanese are quite secretive in their dealings making many details of deals seldomly reported

With the lack of public source documents, finding Japanese "normal" is not going to be easy for the western negotiator. There are only a limited number of other ways to be aware of such business practices, none of which are practical for an opportunistic situation. You can try to source books that explain the internal workings of Japanese businesses and how they interact with one another, but these are few and far between. Of those that

143

you can find, identifying one as a reliable source is another task unto itself. Not many westerners are capable of participating in Japanese-Japanese deals; in particular, it is rare to find a westerner in a Japanese company who is allowed to be part of any domestic (*i.e.*, Japanese) negotiations. It is often hard enough to get involved with international ones. Therefore, finding a credible western author on the subject is virtually impossible. And it is rare to find a Japanese author who wants to make this known to the west.

Another way to find what is the standard business dealing in Japan is to hire your own Japanese staff. This is a bit more helpful except for the fact that, again, they will not know what pieces of the puzzle you require from your western perspective nor will they know what parts of the negotiation play the most important role. Another factor not to be underestimated is the nationalistic factor. Japanese, despite who pays their bill, are hesitant to "betray" their fellow countryman. I've seen it all too often in the Japanese pharmaceutical industry. A small- to mid-sized company would rather deal with the Japanese subsidiary of a multi-national company than with the international headquarters itself. This attitude prevails even if the Japanese subsidiary has nothing to do with the deal at hand. One would think that the subsidiary would respectfully decline any involvement, but they, instead, champion their Japanese brethren to the international headquarters. As the process goes on, it becomes evident where loyalties lie. And it isn't often along corporate lines.

The triple standard has, as its basis, three great assumptions: That you are inferior to the Japanese; that you will never be able to discover what is "normal" in their well veiled national context; and that they have an innate feeling to what is "normal" in your world. What they often fail to realize is that negotiation always proceeds along the lines of relative positions of power. Who needs the business the most? Are there equitable and viable options available to the business prospect? What are the respective potential gains by each party? Answers to these questions help identify who is actually in the driver's seat. It would behoove the lesser of the two to conform to the business practices of the greater so as to provide a smooth and barrier-free process. And more to the point, not to supply a reason to the stronger of the two to look elsewhere for a partner. Nobody will put up with frustration if there is another, equally profitable opportunity waiting in the wings that promises to be a bit more enjoyable.

One interesting aspect of any contract negotiation with the Japanese is their incredible attention to detail. Like a hound ferreting out a fox, they can find almost every extra space, improper indentation, and misspelling along with a host of other grammatical errors. What they may lack, on the other hand, is the understanding of the text itself. As a consequence of this, much of what you have written will be re-phrased. The meanings, you will find, are exactly the same. Now it's in a form that the Japanese can understand. Don't be overly critical of this. While it may not read well or flow like a river, it is something they understand, and that's very important. Nobody—not even you—will sign something you don't understand. Keep the goal firmly fixated in your mind: Sealing the deal.

A cautionary note on this: The language they propose may actually change the meaning and deviate slightly from the writer's original intention. This is because they do not possess an innate feeling for the appropriate use of the vocabulary they've chosen. In many cases, the process of translating from Japanese to English inevitably has them consulting a dictionary. Equally inevitably, the selected word will always be incorrectly used. Other times, the Japanese may be hung up on certain words or phrases from previous agreements. Again, by not knowing the proper usage of such phrases, they will be seemingly be interlined randomly with otherwise well written text.

Going back and correcting this can become tiresome after a while. Generally, asking what legal difference is wrought by their correction will soon put a stop to that. Unfortunately, if their legal staff truly does not understand the text, you have a long row to hoe. To help alleviate this problem—especially as definitive agreements can be quite long—and to avoid spending a disproportionate amount of time on secretarial stuff, ensure your first draft is well suited towards your audience. Remember, your legal counsel consists of native speakers operating in their own field of expertise. They can spend a bit of time and check the draft for unnecessarily convoluted phrases or expressions. While it doesn't always make for a pretty document, you may find that recycling language is one way to decrease the processing time on the part of the Japanese. In the end and again, the Japanese are not going to sign something they do not understand. If this means re-drafting the entire agreement using *Reading for Understanding* level English, then so be it.

What you are going to want to do, and something you should keep in mind as you start drafting documents, is to minimize the time it takes to get from first draft to an executed agreement. Nothing will expedite this as much as a clear and easy to understand draft. The luxury of time is not something you want to grant a Japanese company. This gives them too much time to think and allows for the material situation at hand to change—either more in your favor or more in theirs. Naturally, we all want to get the best financials: Pay as little as possible to get as much as possible, and *vice versa*. But in this scenario, this is a risk you are definitely not going to want to take. If you decide to postpone your decision until the results of the critical test they were running become available, you risk much. The best thing that can happen is that the price gets jacked up. That's fine. We all understand that this is the price you pay for de-risking an opportunity and to increase confidence that the project will be a success. But what many of us do not count on is that suddenly your entire negotiations may be on hold as they approach or re-approach other companies. In this respect, you'll need to decide if you have the heart of a gambler. One path you may want to pursue and one which the Japanese are generally amenable is that of an option agreement.

Once you're satisfied that the document you have created is legally solid and can be grasped by people with limited English skills, it's time to send it off for their comments. I don't imagine anyone on the planet thinks for one minute that it will be accepted as is. There will be a number of changes and this necessarily takes time. When dealing with the Japanese there is not much of a line

147

distinguishing "non-binding" from "binding" documents. Both are, in effect, treated, reviewed and signed as if they were binding. This review process takes quite a great deal of time. It would be a good idea to establish from the very beginning at what points in the negotiation process the Japanese will need to run drafts by senior management. This term, "senior management" can be interpreted as "board members."

A normal internal review process for a draft goes something like this: First, your counterpart will read through it. This will probably be done in parallel with other key members of the business development group. In particular there is oftentimes an individual within that group who liaises directly with other relevant groups in the company, especially the legal group. This person's input and cooperation is vital to an expeditious review.

This is where the real bottleneck takes place: The legal section of most Japanese companies is undermanned and over taxed. This is nothing new; most legal sections are much the same. The difference here is that the Japanese legal staff do not necessarily have enough experience with the English language and may not be all that familiar with US/EU contract law. If you are lucky, the staff member that will be working on your agreement will have passed the bar somewhere in the US and so have at least a superficial understanding of how things should work. Still, this experience may be ancient history to them at this point in their careers and the document will, most likely, still take some time to decipher. If this is not the case and they are seeing this for the first time, you better sit and get comfortable because you're really going to have to wait.

Once everyone has had a chance to peruse the document, they will need to meet and discuss their comments and proposed changes. This means they need to find a time during the course of the day or work week where they all have mutually free time. Not always an easy thing. Chances are they will need two meetings: one to discuss their comments and propose changes and the second to review the actual pen and ink changes made on the document. It could be that if the number of changes is small, this could be consolidated into one meeting, but if the volume of amendments is large, it will need to be two separate gatherings.

After this small group is all aligned one with the other, the document will need some management buy-in at some senior level. How far up the chain it needs to go depends on at which stage you are. There will be a time somewhere in the back-and-forth exchanges of proposals and counterproposals that it will need to be run all the way up the corporate flagpole. That is, the business development group will pitch it to the board to ensure that the negotiations are on the right track. This, again, takes time, as the entire board will need to be available to review this. One characteristic of the Japanese system is that if there is no convenient time or regularly scheduled board meetings, each member can be approached individually for his approval. This approach might shave a couple of days off the process.

The whole thing, from receipt of the draft to the sending of the counterdraft, takes at least two weeks under normal conditions. A very special case may see this reduced to around one week, but this occurs so seldom it

149

is neither of any real value to mention here nor one to be relied upon no matter what your counterpart maybe telling you. In actual practice, I recommend allowing three weeks per turn.

Knowing that a full turn of a draft—that is, proposal to counterproposal—is going to eat up about four to six weeks of time, you can get a relatively good idea of how long it's going to take to complete the whole process. From start line (term sheet) to finish line (executed definitive agreement), I have rarely seen anything faster than six months. Historically, nine may be a better estimate. Depending on the cultural hurdles, how far apart your terms are at the onset, the complexity of the Japanese management structure, the difficulty of the English in a first draft, and what other projects are going on internally at both organizations, this whole thing could take the better part of a year or more.

How can you reduce this time? Face-to-face meetings held at strategic points during the negotiation process can short-circuit a lot of the red tape and you can find that a great deal more is accomplished in a two-day period than in a two-month period. The key to these meetings is to identify the major stumbling blocks and address these rate limiting factors first. To make the most of the meeting, an agenda clearly outlining the key issues should be sent well in advance. This allows the Japanese to set up access to their senior management during the meeting thereby enabling real-time responses rather than the traditional, circuitous ones. Go prepared to make decisions on the spot. This means getting adequate operational instructions from your management and knowing clearly where your limitations are on the items to be discussed and what leeway may exist. Smart money will hold the meeting at a point where the Japanese are due to give a counterproposal and NOT with you going there and responding to a proposal from them. If you plan to go with amended terms in hand, you are going to waste a lot of time and a lot of money. The only thing you will accomplish is (hopefully) solidifying your relationship, something very important to the Japanese and not to be underrated but perhaps not worth the financial and personnel onus that a trip to Japan often entails. Westerners are much better at thinking on their feet and our business models are such where we do not need to consult with half the company before being able to respond to a proposal. By going and receiving their next turn of the document, you will have ensured in the best way you can that the Japanese have already fully staffed the latest draft and are going to the table with a purpose.

It is important at face-to-face meetings with the Japanese to push for frequent breaks. The Japanese are marathon meeting machines and can sit all day without a bio-break. Prior to the start of the session, you may want to appoint someone, preferably from your own team, as the break-meister. As I have already mentioned, breaks can be an invaluable opportunity for both teams to discuss among themselves what has transpired thus far and to strategize for the next session. For the Japanese, it is far more useful than for westerners: This gives them a chance to run up to their manager and brief him in real time on the negotiations. The manager can then give immediate feedback and this will better keep the negotiation on track and keep them more closely aligned to what senior managers want. This translates into a shorter review period later, once you've gone. It also gives them time to catch up; that is, to collectively get on the same page as to what has transpired thus far.

Some logistical items to prepare: Ask for the use of a separate meeting room during breaks. This is a place can act as a safe zone where you can review what has happened and adjust your negotiation strategy if needs be. Request that sufficient coffee and—more importantly—water is on hand. After an international flight you will be drowsy in the early afternoon (thus the coffee) and borderline dehydrated (ergo the water).

Using a liquid plasma projector and making corrections to a common draft as you move article-by-article through the agreement eliminates the word smithing that tends to go on post discussion. Agreeing on language that accommodates you and makes the Japanese happy can be more than half the battle.

Working lunches are both common and desirable. Taking off to a restaurant is time consuming and distracting. Coming back to the table fully loaded presents unneeded difficulties in getting re-focused *vis-à-vis* food coma. In drafting your agenda, suggest a working lunch if one hasn't already been proposed. The Japanese also favor this approach and are all too willing to comply. The exception to this is if a key decision-maker is not available for a dinner and can only make a lunch. In this case, you'll have to do the out-to-lunch thing, but the relationship building that goes on more than justifies the disruption in the negotiation process. Remember, this guy will have to sign off on the work you're doing. Anything that you can do to grease those bureaucratic wheels now always pays dividends later.

One footnote: If you are going the working lunch route, load up on breakfast. Small to mid-sized Japanese companies really don't know what foreigners eat for lunch and so you'll get a range of fares. Sandwiches are popular. Be forewarned, these are not of the caliber you get from a coroner NYC deli. Japanese sandwiches are crustless slices of thin bread with filling only where slices have been cut in half (diagonally). This provides you with about a mouthful of goodies and the rest is starch. All told, one sandwich is about as thick as one slice of SunBeam bread. A green salad, or a potato salad may be offered as sides.

Pizza is often a choice as the Japanese identify this delicacy with US culture. But just as we alter Japanese food to fit our culture, so, too, do the Japanese adapted other international cuisines to their own. This means that you can expect a wider range of topping, including mayonnaise, fruit, unknown vegetables, seaweed, fish and the ever-ubiquitous culinary additive, corn. Generally, all on a cracker-like crust.

If the Japanese are uncertain what to order they'll order a "bento," or box lunch. These are top-of-the-line lunches and can cost up to $50.00 each. They are also an adventure-in-a-box for westerners who are still cutting their teeth, as it were, on Japanese food. With the higher end *bento*s, few things may be recognizable. Ready yourself. If this deters you or if you just want to play it safe, work out these details with their point of contact in advance.

Although you'll want to make use of every minute you

can, don't start too early or run too late. Set boundaries to the extent you can on your day. Again, the Japanese do not function well in the early hours and can burn the midnight oil long past the time vampires hit the sack. Moderation is the best use of your energy. Further to this, try not to get sidetracked. It is easy enough especially when there are a number of interrelated articles in an agreement. The two obvious disadvantages to going off on a tangent are: (i) inefficient use of your time; and (ii) your Japanese counterparts have difficulty following such jumps in the English language. They will soon be lost as evidenced by the look their faces. It will take them no small amount of time, either then and there or after you have gone home, to get re-centered. This may end up being counterproductive as the whole idea of the face-to-face meeting is to save time.

Limit your visit to two days. This gives you time to get to and from Japan in one week and gives the Japanese time to have all the necessary after-action reviews in the same week. This is a good idea because everything will still be fresh in their minds. Try not to have a meeting on the day that you leave Japan. Generally, if you are traveling to the States *via* an American or European carrier, your flight leaves in the late afternoon; for Europe a little earlier. If you're flying Japanese carriers, the times are a bit earlier than that, at around noon. Use the early mornings of those days to get to the airport and clear immigration and customs. Once on the concourse, use the hour or two before your flight to draft and send the meeting minutes off to your counterpart. As with all your meetings, getting the minutes into the hands of the Japanese does not leave much to their imaginations and serves to head off misinterpretations.

On the subject of "how" to negotiate, I'm sure many out there have either had plenty of homegrown experience or have read one of the many "how-to" books that have inundated the market over the past years. The suggestions and helpful tips that are supplied in those manuals are largely based on the assumption that you are all operating from the same negotiating manual. That is, there is a common thread that runs through each person when squaring off across the negotiating table. For lack of a better phrase, I like to call it a common "business culture." Naturally, there are differences, and these widen as you move out of the US and into Europe. But, by and large, the foundation is pretty much the same. Now when you move into the Orient, you can brain dump all the nuances and finer techniques that score points in a western setting. Without that common business culture, the words you use and approach you take suddenly do not wield the impact that they would have otherwise in a more home-grown situation.

I have all too often seen westerners leave the negotiating table in Japan expressing a wide spectrum of emotions ranging from frustration to amusement. But whatever the flavor of the day, one thought, in particular, is prevalent: "How do I get these guys to see (my) reason?" But it would be like trying to teach Newtonian physics to Martians. There is no frame of reference. What is important to you may seem like nonsense to them. Nothing could be further from the truth than when an American is trying to reason with a Japanese and *vice versa*.

155

We're back at the theory of "opposites" here. You are convinced that going left is the only logical course of action, but your Japanese counterpart, looking at the same situation, feels only an equal compulsion to turn right.

This comes, in a way, from a perversion of Abraham Maslow's hierarchy of needs. We, in the west are bottom-line driven; that is, we are looking to expand business through profit. We understand that the reasons for doing anything in business is to first and foremost survive, then to bring compensation to shareholders and investors. For example, research into pharmaceuticals is done solely for the purpose to bring a drug to the market that will provide a certain level of income to finance future research and provide a tidy dividend for the shareholders. Everyone in the organization—from the guy who washes out the beakers to the Chief Scientific Officer—is aware of this goal. It is rare that a pharmaceutical company spends the purported $1 billion in development expenses just to give the drug away for free. It just doesn't happen. And I use the pharmaceutical industry only as an example. The same holds true for whatever industry you look at, whether it be electronics, automobiles, processed foods…whatever. No public company gives anything away for free. What becomes important to us above and beyond these basic needs depends on where we are in the evolution of the company.

We can draw a modified hierarchy of "business needs" that reflects what western companies generally focus on and what Japanese companies at the same stage are focusing on. The figure below reflects the western companies' urge for survival, whether through private

156

investors or through a public offering. We all innately realize that without cash, we crumple and no matter how good a product we may have our business goes under. Japanese, on the other hand, are not all that concerned with the operational needs. Traditionally, the banking system has floated business long past time when they would have been insolvent in any other country.

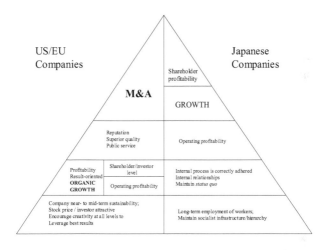

The Japanese are far more concerned to ensure its employees have lifetime employment. The *daimyo-samurai* sub-culture is still pervasive and this is still looked upon by corporate magnates as a primary responsibility, no matter what the cost to the company. Even in this day and age, you rarely hear of companies out and out firing people. Oh yes, you can read a number of articles about this company cutting X number of jobs, or that company closing Y number of facilities. But in virtually all cases, there is a soft landing for those directly affected. Generally, the reductions in jobs are due to natural and corporate wide attrition and early retirements incentives, with early retirement in Japan being 55 years old—a very close age to the mandatory age of 60. Cross-investments between banking conglomerates and companies has long staved off having to resort to cutthroat economics so prevalent in the rest of the world. A subtle difference between capitalism and socialism.

Once the need for survivability has been met and no longer becomes a daily or frequent worry, westerners focus on getting money back into the company. This we often refer to as running in the black. Once this can be attained, the next logical extension is to divert profits back to the investors or shareholders. After all, they, in effect, own the company.

Japanese, on the other hand, look to ensure there is a harmonious environment in which they can corporately operate. Rules and procedures take precedence over success and profits. Internal relations are nurtured and forged. Consensus and round-robin decision-making engines are built. The idea here is that a well-oiled machine, with each piece functioning in unison with the rest, will ultimately be a productive, powerful and, in business, profitable entity. This takes its toll in time and money—both "non-concerns" for the Japanese.

As westerners move up the ladder and as our financial well-being is more secured—at least for a foreseeable future—we begin to focus on a corporate identity. This process probably starts farther down the pyramid, but really blossoms here. We now have the money and the moxie to become the ideal we've dreamed about from our inception. Reputation becomes all-important. Brand recognition is stressed, and quality over competitors—real or perceived—is touted. We put back into the communities we take from. We try become "Eco-friendly" and go to great lengths to show John Q. Public that we are one of him. We are not greedy, profit mongers at his expense, but rather we are adding value to his lifestyle and thus imparting to him a service and benefit he would not otherwise enjoy.

A brief aside: We talk about improving corporate reputation and image. For the Japanese, reputation trumps profitability every time. Successful decisions are made more from the ability of a company to have some sort of bragging rights the deal brings rather than the money they stand to make. This strive for status is, perhaps, the single, most effective arrow in your quiver. The better you can showcase what the deal will do to their standing amongst their peers—both corporately and in their university circles—the more likely you are in signing a good deal quickly. As you convey this to your Japanese partner, be sure to do so subtly; its always more effective if the Japanese come to the conclusion on their own and think it was their idea.

At this stage in the pyramid, we become a bit more selective in our business undertaking. And rightly so. We can afford to be picky. This attitude bleeds over into the deals we subsequently pursue and the conditions and criteria to which these are held. But at the same point in corporate growth, a Japanese company is now looking to make some cash, at least to maintain its operating expenses. Now that the company is finally at a point where all systems are in place and everyone is holding hands and singing "Kumbaya" they are ready to move as one into the money zone. By knowing where your potential partner lies in comparison with what strata you inhabit can be invaluable in pushing all the right buttons to get them to see the deal in terms that are important to them.

Contract negotiation is a lengthy process at best. The things that make the difference between taking a year or more to complete and being able to wrap things up in six months are well worth identifying. Playing the game on your own terms but using their rules certainly goes a long way in abbreviating the timeline. Recognize that what is important to you may not even be on their radar screen. Shift strategy to simultaneously get what you want while satisfying their needs. This is nothing that takes years to master. You do, though, need to adhere to the P^3 principle: Patience, perseverance and planning. And plenty of doses of each.

A successful contract, a signed agreement, and a solidified relation is the result more of your ability to see their side than theirs to see yours. At first this may strike you as unfair. A westerner is, generally, better equipped to view a broader range of possibilities and to have a greater tolerance for different ideas. Briefly, westerners are more open-minded. They have to be, living in a fragmented culture with a potpourri of people. While we are tolerant to a great degree of diversity, we are not tolerant of narrow-mindedness. A bit of a dichotomy to be sure, but a real issue when dealing with the Japanese. Keep your emotions, especially this frustration, in check. Wear your best poker face and avoid eye rolling and grimaces. Control your emotions without being emotionless.

Foremost, keep your wits about you. In Japanese negotiations it is easy to get blind-sided if you get too carried away with the progress you may be making. In this context, progress may be illusory.

As a last reality check, remind yourself periodically what your end game is: Is it to provide a good business opportunity first to your company and then to the Japanese company; or is it something only that inures to your benefit.

Caveat Emptor

These two words should echo in your mind during your entire exposure to any Japanese company; they are unpredictable and often exhibit a great deal of instability at senior management. By this, I mean that the policies of today are the histories of tomorrow. Reasons for such shifts can vary but many stem from a reorganization of subordinate units in the wake of a regime change. The changes may seem outwardly to have little to do with logic or common sense. Often, they occur to accentuate a change in leadership, a leadership that can change every three to five years. It is helpful to understand where your negotiations fall in the cycle. To wit, will you need to endure a change in senior management, and, if you do, how will that affect your potential business dealings with the company?

There has been a long-standing theory by the Japanese that they are physiologically different from all other *homo sapiens* on the planet Earth. Whether this theory stemmed from observations made from a cultural or a genetic point of view, I cannot say. What is apparent though, is that dealing with Japanese is a singularly unique experience not shared even by their Asian neighbors. It could be due to their long period of isolation. Or it could be due to their ongoing efforts to maintain racial purity.

Foreigners, by and large, are considered uncouth, uncultured, uncivilized creatures. Asians are looked upon as truly primitive and "dirty," while westerners are labeled as a people who would do anything for a buck. This old guard attitude still purveys many of the hallowed halls of Japanese corporate headquarters. It is slowly changing, but until this generation of leaders passes, the change will not be complete. Perhaps even then enough of the old school philosophy will have been passed down that a massive titration will be needed before any discernable change takes place. If that turns out to be the case, it could be a very long while, indeed, before corporate Japan can do business on equal footing with its foreign counterparts.

As with any self-contained system, the catalyst for quick change is catastrophe. For the Japanese, who have mainly relied on the production of goods to stay afloat economically, this may come in the form of China. The sleeping dragon is stirring and attracting investment from a wide range of international businesses. The fear for the Japanese is what happens when China's intellectual property laws catch up with its desire to be an economic powerhouse. This would allow manufacturers to take advantage of cheap semi-skilled labor and for service industries to flourish unimpeded by knock-offs. High end items like pharmaceutical and computer software would enjoy the protection of the state which would encourage the mother companies to invest in the Chinese

163

infrastructure. Assuming that only 10% of the Chinese population would be in a position to benefit from this surge of capitalism, the numbers would still be buoyant enough to outstrip Japanese production and consumption.

Another manufacturing powerhouse that has emerged in Asia is Korea. Televisions, cars, and electronic devices are booming in this country. In hard markets companies such as LG, Samsung, Hyundai, and KIA have risen to the levels of Sony, Toshiba, Toyota, and Honda.

As these countries increase their share of market and share of voice internationally, the Japanese economy is becoming more and more marginalized. An option to do business in China or Korea where the frustrations felt by foreigners are considerably less than those felt with Japan Inc. is an attractive and motivating factor in shifting business dealings from Japan to these other countries.

Yet, the Japanese are either nonplussed by these developments or are ignorant of them. What do I mean?

You may be on the brink of signing a deal only to find out that you have been leveraged against another Japanese company. You may be informed that there will be an undisclosed delay in signing of your agreement, or that the Japanese simply cannot sign the agreement at this time. Leveraging is not uncommon. *Au contraire*, it is prudent. The difference is that we in the west are generally transparent about the process. How else do we get the best deal? Popping surprises rarely works. The Japanese, though, take a little different approach.

The Japanese view deals among themselves as the gold standard. These domestic deals are preferable to mixing it up with foreigners. And, to some extent, this is true of any country. The difference is that, while it may be preferable to keep business within one's own kind, it is not the ultimate deciding factor in the west. Inside Japan, however, to partner with another Japanese company is the single driving factor. Only when this cannot be achieved will a small- to mid-sized company open its doors to foreigners. And even then, they will employ every means at their disposal to use the relationship and information generated by its interacting with you to persuade their Japanese candidates to change their "no's" to "yes's" about partnering.

All too often, westerners enter into the land of the rising sun harboring stereotypes of the Japanese. Where these preconceptions arise from are mostly fabrications of westerners and not an accurate representation of the actual situation in Japan. First, there is no such thing as "honor" in Japan, at least as we have had portrayed to us. This is a word of storybooks and movies. This bushido code vanished long, long ago—if it ever existed. And even then, "honor" was a term used to get people to do something they didn't want to do. Like kill themselves. A sense of fairness and the qualities we would equate to chivalry simply do not exist. In many ways, the Japanese are more self-serving than us westerners. At least we are honest about this and harbor no delusions about our end game. "Honor" as a word or an ideal does not appear in the language, culture, or history.

Ethics are also rarely encountered. A sense of fair play has never been adopted and, as I have already mentioned, double/triple standards are frequently employed. A "do unto others then run away" attitude purveys all aspects of

Japanese business. This may be part and parcel due to the lack of a wide spread religious influence within the country. Much of the principles we, as westerners, regard as standard derive their origins in the Christian ethos. In Japan, Buddhism is reported as the prevailing religious doctrine, but in practice only the elderly pay a great deal of attention to it. Even if this doctrine would have some impact on the business culture, Buddhism as it exists in Japan, is only loosely based on the religion as it came from India and China. It has been revised to fit the Japanese expectation of life and even if it were applied to business would still be egocentric.

Trust is a word tossed around like so much spare change to a beggar. The Japanese steadfastly believe that trust is something that only the Japanese are capable of and that all foreigners are races of betrayers. When they begin negotiations with western companies, Japanese—especially the entrenched hardliners at the seats of power—think nothing of breaking "trust" with their counterparts. The prevailing reason for this is that the Japanese do not operate under the assumption that trust has been established.

Negotiating in good faith does not have the same meaning to Japanese that it does to us. Yes, "good faith" is a ubiquitous line in almost any agreement, but care needs to be taken when invoking this phrase. They and we are not operating off the same sheet of music. To the Japanese, "good faith" means that they are being accommodated.

You as the westerner need to bear in mind the difference in this "good faith" approach. Remember that the Japanese are interpreting this term in the context of what they know, which is rarely the same as what you know. Assumptions are the killers here. We tend to believe that when a company enters into negotiations for a definitive agreement, they have the intention to sign it. At the very least they have the intention to pursue until it can go no further. What is not intended, is a professional development exercise for a party's legal and business groups. This may or may not be a vision shared by your Japanese counterparts. It is important to lay all the cards out on the table from Jump Street. By this I mean that, depending on the situation—and I recommend you take nothing for granted no matter who tells you what—you may want to preface in-depth negotiations with a binding memorandum of understanding or an exclusivity agreement. If you can't agree on this, then you may want to re-evaluate spending the time and money and reputation pursing a deal with this company. Sadly, such documents are still necessary safeguards when doing business with the Japanese in the 21st century.

"Reasons" you give for doing or not doing something are very often labeled "excuses." Turn around, however and again, is not fair play. The Japanese intolerance for excuses does not extend to its own very ample supply. These "reasons," instead are deemed facts or self-evident truths.

One way to counter a large number of these situations is to improve your memory. Better yet, keep copious notes. As you move forward, these will prove invaluable in identifying double/triple standards and in pointing out gaps in information or lapses in communication that serve

167

the Japanese as a basis for a particular action. Share these with your potential partner and establish transcripts as sources to be referenced should you confront a situation that seems in contradiction with the one you feel to be reality. It may later be tossed out or marginalized, but that tells you something about with who you're dealing

But nothing will prevent the Japanese from raining on your parade. The internal system of the company is prejudiced against western companies in several ways. First, there is the corporate culture. This will almost always consist of an "old-school" management whereby maintaining an inflated and self-perceived importance takes precedence over company profitability and image. Maintaining relations with peers in the same industry occupies a higher place in the business than does deal making. There often is no penalty for throwing away opportunities. There are penalties for failing at an established undertaking, but none for getting to a hair's breadth away from signing and then chucking it all away just so a university classmate at a competing company can review the opportunity.

In the balance, and like the US and EU, there are rules and laws governing certain businesses that are publicly owned. In this respect, a public corporation cannot out-and-out lie to you about a business opportunity. Let me re-phrase that: A corporation _shouldn't_ out-and-out lie to you about an opportunity. They may do so, thinking that there's no way you will ever find out. And even if you do there's damn all you can do about it. And to a certain extent, they're right. It is not often that a Japanese court of law sides with a foreign firm, whatever the law books say. As a western company there's very little recourse you can take against a Japanese company on their home turf. Keep this in mind as you determine a contract's governing law.

A deal may fall flat in its final stages. You may think things are progressing along well and at a good clip when suddenly your business counterpart tells you, with face smiling, that their senior management has reviewed the opportunity and has decided to forego it. This is the point where you discover that the person you've been dealing with for the last few months wields no power in his own organization. When he pitched the deal internally, he did not have enough influence to gather a positive consensus. Again, there is little you can do except stand with mouth agape at all your wasted time, effort, and money.

Be careful with delivering ultimatums. These tend to be viewed by the Japanese as "bluffs." What they fail to realize is that ultimatums are, well, just that: Ultimatums. There is no going back. In that way it is much like dying. You can rue your decision from the beyond, but what you can't do is have another lease on life. So before saying you are going to walk away, make sure your best alternative to a negotiated agreement (BATNA) is firmly in place and, if needed, use it. Turn, walk away, and don't look back.

Now, in the case where the Japanese return to you and vigorously petition for a resurrection in talks, I would think that the "negotiations" on your part are over. You just give your final offer and they can take it or leave it. With a solid "Plan B" in the works, you just plain and simple don't need the hassle.

Something to keep in mind as you move ahead with

partnering is the decision-making process; in particular, the length of time needed for a final decision in the Japanese forum. As a rule, the Japanese are snail slow at saying "yes" to an opportunity. Getting a "no" reply is not all that much shorter. It is difficult to judge the status of a deal based on the turn around time of communication. Consensus building is a time-consuming process subjected to individual schedules. A week is not a luxury. On the other hand, an exorbitant amount of time should throw flags up in your direction. Feedback from a Japanese firm saying that it will take another couple weeks to check a few lines of text should be suspect. At this point, you may wish to establish direct communication rather than going through e-mails or letters. The closer to a "live" communiqué you get, the closer to the truth you will find yourself. While a telephone call can be effective, a visit can be deciding albeit expensive. The offer of one is also telling. If they balk, it may be an indication that things are going badly.

You will find that the amount of backbone you encounter will be directly proportional to the distance you get from the source. Kind of like the gravitational force equation. All too many times decision-making committees sit around the table and internally discuss what they are going to do and how they are going to put so-and-so in their place. They decide that "X" royalty is the line in the sand and should you not toe that line, then they'll send you packing. The senior staff works themselves up in a lather on how they are not going to bow to any more demands nor are they going to concede any more points. These meeting can escalate the righteousness of their position even if, and in most cases when, there is no hard-core facts to back up that position. It can become a thunderous, corporate, and nationalistic rally. But the momentum they generate is one of "topping." Each consecutive speaker needs to make an even more outlandish proposal than the previous one until the whole committee is clearly—and even by their standards—out of hand. Once they are full of themselves—sated to overflowing—the meeting ends and they send the BDL crew out to the front lines.

This corporate momentum quickly abates as soon as you walk into the room. You and facts, a little thing that serves to deflate the world constructed behind their closed corporate doors. Seeing the formation of the strategy and the execution is an experience that is not easily explained. You run the gamut of emotions: Confusion, doubt, audacity, amazement, and embarrassment. Even the Japanese BDL representatives, when they hear it coming out of their mouths, tend to cringe. A polite rejection from your side usually puts these proposals to bed.

The main reason for the "rally" and the "proposal" and the "roll over" is that most times mid-sized companies don't know what is normal international industry practice. They are floundering and walking like a blind man in a maze. Learning by trial and error.

Face-to-face is the best way to stare them down, so to speak. If you reach a point similar to what I'm describing here, it may be time for a personal visit. But remember, you've got to get your foot in the door and keep it there. Too much perceived bullying will have your potential Japanese partner scrambling for someone else.

Now it is exactly because they have no idea of what is standard or how to value something that leads to tangential changes in policies. It can be a bit frightening, particularly when you feel that you are close and the deal is just beyond. You've invested a great deal of time, money and assets to get this far and to be suddenly snubbed and left out in the cold is something that you would, understandably, prefer not to happen. But it sometimes does.

Japanese firms are not very good at fronting their products to western companies. They simply don't know how. All too often you will be on the receiving end of some presentation, or some sales pitch that is passé or obsolete. This is the precedence thing kicking-in. They use the same western techniques used on them in the last deal they tried to hammer together. All too often, that deal was more than half a decade ago and didn't get very far in the first place. This last element may go a long way to explain sudden down shifts in quality you may experience as you move through the different stages of a deal. But because they can't seem to advertise—for lack of a better word—the opportunity, responses from preferred partners don't roll in until the word spreads a bit more. This is the danger in being the early bird here. The worm is liable to get ripped right from your mouth

Instead, convey the immediate value of the deal. Anticipate more attractive candidates moving in at the last minute. Be ready for them and have a rebuttal on-hand. Be sure that somewhere in your strategy is the training module, "Why it's better to partner with a western company rather than a Japanese one." This is essential.

Particularly, you will need to show that language and culture are not hurdles, but are well within the confines of the manageable. These are tools that can be used to help one grow as a company and can be used as stepping-stones in taking one's place on the international scene. They are tools to attract other future foreign business and serve as good training for their employees. These are all things that Japanese companies can relate to and cozy up to and, if presented properly, can also serve to advance you in the deal you are pursuing.

Bottom line: Expect the unexpected. Beware of things that are too good to be true. You know...all the usual doom-and-gloom stuff. You want to consider working subtle safeguards in your binding documents as you slowly progress towards a definitive agreement. At the very least you will get some idea of senior management's present school of thought to suddenly committing the asset in a different strategic direction. This does not prevent them from waking one morning and give away such-and-such an opportunity to a Japan colleague.

Whatever the strategy, whatever the tactics you employ, make sure that you cover your ass and that these tactics are designed and executed with those all-too-familiar Latin words of warning in mind: *Caveat Emptor*.

Language

I would be serious remiss if I did not, at some point, address the language issue. It is something that our European brothers know a great deal more about than us colonials. The use of language—specifically, English—has been a result of a number of items that, had they occurred in a different order or were they separated by a few more generations, would not now be a force to reckon with.

As Americans, we often, if not always, take for granted that the peoples of the world speak flawless English. In our nation's history, we are only now faced with the dilemma that more of our country's inhabitants do not speak English as a native tongue than do. English is still overwhelmingly the language of business both inside and outside of America. Like Porsche, there is no substitute.

There is a relatively large and disproportionate number of Americans that have never left the shores of their homeland. Some have traveled to Mexico or even ventured to Canada, but the vast majority do not have a significant foreign experience. In short, they hold on to a perspective of life as viewed through the American media and the American cinematic phenomenon. This makes us a bit language insensitive, especially those who live outside the very few true cosmopolitan US cities.

We really do not know how to interact with foreign speakers and tend to associate volume with understanding. If a listener does not understand us, we begin to raise our voices, escalating into a screaming rage. The vocabulary and grammar tend to remain similar if not the exact same. It's as if there is an innate "English" center in everyone's brain that can be accessed only by pummeling the receiver with high amplitude sound waves.

Now, from an armchair position, we can all ogically rationalize that this is not the case. But in an actual, real life situation where we are confronted by poor English speakers, logic vaporizes. Emotions tend to take precedence. Ergo, the yelling. Watching from the outside, no matter what your linguistic background, this approach to forced understanding appears to border on the comical. But for many, having never been on the receiving side of this type of language exchange, it seems like a very natural reflex. Coming up with more effective ways to breach this language barrier is not so obvious.

Europeans are generally more sensitive to language. They tend to need an more of an arsenal of different languages or dialects to conduct business on a day-to-day basis. Europe has always been a collection of separate states economically linked to one another. It has only been in relatively recent history that they have banded together under the umbrella of a European Union. But if one were to trace the history of the continent, it is plain to see how closely the events in one country affect those in another. Balance of power—and by extension trade—has ever been of utmost importance to western Europeans. As each country has industrialized post-World War II, they have grown economically intertwined. In fact, the typical job interview techniques employed by companies that need salesmen or engineers to service a broad European clientele would begin in a native language and then arbitrarily switch languages as the interview progressed. Spanish, French, and German were mainstays, but often the deciding factor was the interviewee's fluency in English.

While it is always preferable to speak to somebody in their own language, English has long been used as a fallback language. This is more due to history than to the ease and convenience of the language itself. English colonization during the 17th, 18th, and 19th centuries has spread the tongue across the globe. Where regional, tribal leaders once prevailed, the English settlers brought unification. Without English, several African nations along with world powers, such as India, would still be a patchwork of regional tribes. A unifying communication system allowed them to consolidate power bases, establish trade and an ensuing economy, and take their rightful places on the world stage.

It could've been any language that did this. If not for Nelson and Wellesley, it could've been French. Had the Armada been a bit more successful against Drake, it could've been Spanish. It just turned out to be English.

Until the "war to end all wars," World War I, was

fought, America held predominantly to a *laissez-faire* policy. In over simplified terms, they believed in "live and let live." Yet, whether for good or bad, America has emerged as the dominating power of the 20th and, so far, the 21st centuries. Economically, there are no other people on the planet that spend more and save less. This consumer addiction has made the US the target for virtually every business in the world. No matter how large or how small, every one aspires to be a success in the US marketplace. Without the average American spending so much on a number of useless things, the economies of lesser countries would be in peril, or nonexistent. This is something that we freely acknowledge and something that, consciously or no, we use to strong-arm nations around the world to toe our line. Side with the US or suffer the loss of the world's largest consumer market.

And having to learn and use English is a large part of that. We expect the businessmen in France to speak English. We expect the businessmen in Italy to speak English. We expect the businessmen in Estonia to speak English. And to speak it with a fluency and naturalness of a native. It is a sad thing to see, from an ex-patriate point of view, how little Americans perceive of the world around them. Yes, we are more informed due to satellite network news broadcasted 24/7, but we fail to really "see" the cultures that are being projected on our TV screens, or understand the "foreigners" that we interface with at conferences or business functions.

Knowing that many of the Americans who will engage in business with the Japanese do not possess international experience, I offer a crash course on dealing with Japanese

177

in English. It boils down to one basic premise: Do everything slowly. In conversations, if you speak slowly and respond slowly, and pause between listening and speaking, your chances of having to do something just once increases. As a monolingual people, we should keep the language rocks in our pockets and not start hurling them the first chance we get at the glass windows of Japanese business. In whatever way you choose to communicate, remember that you are not addressing academia, you are trying to conduct business in a language that is as far from English as is Martian-ese.

In the Venn diagram of English and Japanese, the subset is the null set. Yes, certain western business words have crept their way into the Japanese vocabulary, and, yes, the Japanese businessman will be pulling out some words and phrases he has learned from his NHK home study course, but beware: They may not have the same meaning or even a similar pronunciation. Furthermore, there is no way that you will be able to revolve the intricacies of a business deal around these handful of words.

Now, if you are one of those people who are naturally loquacious and articulate, slow it down and dumb it down. Remember the goal: To ink a deal in as little time as possible, and to establish and maintain a good working relationship with your future partner. This is not going to happen if you are having trouble communicating on a very superficial level.

And the Japanese will make it as tough on you as possible. Not out of any sense of sabotage or ill-directed purpose, but because that's how the system happens to work. All too often the BDL groups are the sanctuaries of

178

the corporate misfits—especially if the company is one of the many "research boutiques" for which Japan is so famous—or infamous. This means that their basis in everything—English and business alike—stems from their tenure as scientists rather than as global corporate citizens. We in the States realize to some degree that the motivations that drive researchers are vastly different than those that drive businessman. Curiosity and philanthropy do not pay the light bills. Cash does. Cash comes either through the generosity of others *vis-à-vis* endowments, or through profitability in the market place. In other words: Sales. And profitable sales only come through a defined corporate system that eliminates inefficiencies and maintains focus on what is marketable.

In your communications with the Japanese firm with whom you'd like to do business, English will inevitably be your base language. I have already given my opinion on the use of translators and consultants. You do better without the majority of them. As a recap: stick to second generation Japanese (*ni-sei*) translators—they've grown up speaking both languages in a (usually) multi-cultural environment; use consultants as an introductory tool only and do not rely on them as a negotiation tool.

Don't lose track of how difficult it is for even the best of the Japanese to maneuver around in a foreign language, especially English. Keep in mind, too, that languages in general are more than just words. They are a culmination of the history of a race. It is a verbal representation of the culture; a reflection of the morals and ethos of a people. That's all real hard to absorb in the six years that one studies a language in junior and senior high schools. As a

179

frame of reference, imagine being air-dropped deep into the Congo with nothing but the clothes on your back and your good looks. Your goal is to navigate to a friendly port in one piece. This is what it is like for the poor souls sitting across from you during your negotiation session in Japan. Except instead of getting to a safe harbor, they are trying just to get through the day.

Now knowing that, in business, we are not an overly compassionate people and that we conform to the dog-eat-dog mentality needed to act as the corporate gladiator and crush your enemies, vanquish the weak and reign supreme in the business arena, I fully anticipate that some individuals will take what we have discussed thus far as a means to railroad the Japanese company into crippling terms and conditions. My advice: Use this linguistic advantage to guide and direct the negotiations rather than to pummel your counterparts into submission. Should the Japanese catch on to underhanded, duplicitous ways, you've just lost what is most important in both the East and West: The trust factor. I cannot delineate—and will not presume to dictate—what policies your firm has with respect to negotiation tactics and strategies, but I would like to offer a sound age-old business postulate that I would hope you consider in your dealings with the Japanese: *If you are in business for good business, making money will be a natural by-product. If you are in business to just make money, then you are going to go broke.*

Japan and Venture Capital

As one might expect from a culture as conservative and tight with money as the Japanese, venture capital funds and venture capital companies are a rarity. They account for only a sliver of the corporate activity domestically. It is interesting to note that new companies in general, despite where the funding for it comes from, are an anomaly. There is a great unwritten rule that equates longevity with success. This success is not measured by a balance sheet but by using the same yardstick that gives older people more money than younger. The fact that a company has persevered for a period of time is a testimony to its commitment to its workers and to the industry. Profits and providing quality goods and services play little in the reputation or in the amount of respect a company receives.

Money to supply operating cash has never been a problem in Japan until recent years. The banks have been a virtual well-spring of never-ending capital. Since companies were failing, and since banks were loaning the money which allowed companies to fund any kind of program—no matter how inane—there has never been any real need in Japan for the venture capital fund. Companies did not consider spin-outs, since they had oodles of yen to fund even the projects that seemingly had no chance of succeeding. There was no thought to offering marginal products to start-up companies—part of this was to avoid the "embarrassment" of having a small, less established company succeed where it failed. Due to the endless flow of cash, companies were broad in their scopes, being more generalists than specialists. Again, with the banks pouring cash into even defunct companies, there has never been a reason to look for alternative sources of financing. Risk was low as long as the coffers were full.

After the burst of the bubble, banks began to wake up to the fact that there wasn't going to be returns on the loans and investments they made in nearly every industrial sector in Japan. Belts started to tighten and companies' commercial activities began to narrow in scope. With this, there were a number of projects across a broad spectrum of industries that were left hanging. The majority of these were hawked both domestically and internationally but the large majority of unlicensed projects went by the wayside.

Even today, the narrowing of foci has not plateaued. But a number of more aggressive individuals have emulated the western venture capital system and have set up funds to invest in one-off opportunities, mostly from academia. Large funds, such as JAFCO (formerly Japan Associated Finance Company) and NIF-SMBC, have grown to the point of being competitive with their western counterparts. While these funds are continually on the lookout for opportunity on their own soil, they still have been known not infrequently to invest in the west.

There are, perhaps, two driving reasons behind this. First, the Japanese by and large are and have always been risk adverse. This is what makes them such strong players in high volume consumer industries, like cars and electronics, and poor players in industries that require enormous leaps of faith, like pharmaceuticals. The second is that licensing something to a VC is akin to "throwing it away"; to be disabused by mercenaries who care little for the product, but only pursue the opportunity in hopes of a wildly lucrative exit before commercialization. Companies would rather covet the asset forever, like an unmarried daughter, than put it into the hands of an uncaring, greedy usurer. So where does this leave you as a venture capitalist or investment banker looking for new projects or products to underwrite?

With plenty of opportunities.

It's just a matter of knowing how to assuage management's fear of the risk and change the way VC is perceived. One of the first hurdles to overcome is to convince them that equity is actually worth something. The Japanese have for so long dealt with cash. Cash is tangible. It is countable. You know how much you have at any time. You can open the drawer or safe or whatever, pull it out, and confirm its existence at any time. Its quantity does not ebb and flow. For the most part it is stable: It does not drastically diminish in value or increase in value based on a relatively few individual opinions or on an elite group's likes or dislikes. In short, it is real and has immediate worth.

Equity, on the other hand, is not. It is an idea, a whim. It is the hope that a value you perceive will be shared by others and that such an agreement will create something out of nothing. Equity is the economic equivalent of religious faith. It is believing without seeing. Such an ethereal concept is not easily grasped by a materialistic culture. This fundamental difference leads to a huge barrier that the VC needs to breach. Japanese companies who are licensing assets out, or who are divesting assets are looking for an immediate return. In other words, cash. Upfronts and development/sales milestones are the mainstay and the idea that all this will be paid in stock somewhere in the future is as imaginable as the physics of space travel would be to a caveman. I can't count the number of times I've heard a western VC fund try to convince a Japanese company that equity will far outweigh any cash prospects.

And the Japanese don't bite. These guys are the personification of the NPV concept; that is, $20 million today is worth more than $200 million five years down the road. A bird in hand and all that. Their culture makes them impervious to adopting a belief system that emphasizes the valuation of nothing into something. Remember that the modern Japanese economy was built on manufacturing. There are no leaps of faiths required for this. You put some raw material in and you get a product out. During the entire process you can see with your own eyes the value being added as the product takes form. Even before the actual production begins, the Japanese know it will work. This concept has been the foundation of their industrial world and the basis for all its

184

business models to date, and you will need to be very clever, indeed, to show how you can determine, arbitrarily, a value to nothing and increase this worth by adding perception. It is difficult for the Japanese to see how this can happen.

And it is, oftentimes, difficult to for westerners to see. Look at all the failed or "undervalued" IPOs over the last decade. To be sure, there have been successful ones, and very lucrative paybacks. But it is a fickle market and subject more to rantings than rationale. The Japanese, taken as a whole, cannot understand this system and if they cannot dissect the workings of something, then that something should be avoided. It goes back to wanting to be in control. Nothing that can decisively impact a business should be left in the hands of fate. You can see this in how they manage industries that are typically risk-oriented businesses. Take, for example, the pharmaceutical industry. Basically, it's a crap shoot. The common practice is to inundate yourself with possibilities and hope that one in ten pays off. If it does, you are profitable. The Japanese tend to run a pharmaceutical company like a chemical company and wait until a very promising candidate can be identified. This, then, is brought forward in the development process. Unfortunately, a thousand different possibilities are discarded along the way, many of which may have actual borne fruit.

Venture capital companies are difficult pitches to make when there is no playbook. You need to discover the specific concerns of the senior management and address these the best you can. Keep in mind that many of theses are smoke screens. No senior level manager is going to want to admit that he doesn't know about an aspect of business. This makes him look a bit inept, especially for his age.

And then there is the suspicious nature that pervades the decision to either divest or license out an opportunity. Suddenly, this asset, which up until now was perceive to have no value, a failure kept alive solely to justify the time and money dumped into it, is attracting the attention of the westerner who specializes in making big money in little time. Perhaps it's worth something after all. Perhaps there is a facet of the asset that has been overlooked. There must be a payback—and a big one to boot. But what is it?

After this revelation, you couldn't pry the asset away from them with a crow bar and a box of dynamite. The company still has no idea the value of what they have, but if the asset is being courted by serious money—they would rather not license or divest it all than to let it go. You will have to pay and pay dearly. But how? Venture capital does not work in ready cash but in promises. This is a selling problem the westerner faces. How to pay Wednesday for a hamburger today. Depending on the company and the position of the product or asset you are pursuing will largely determine what kinds of hoops you need to jump through. Before engaging in any of this be sure yourself that it is all worth the time and effort. It is a lot of work and a lot of persuasion to get where you want to go.

Unique Problems in VC

I call these unique in the sense of how they apply to a Japanese firm, but the same situations and problems described here may very well be present in homegrown venture capital companies as well. In that sense, they are not unique at all.

First and foremost is selling the idea of equity to your future Japanese licensor/divestor. This is something based on an intangible element and a leap of faith; neither of which the Japanese are very adept. But this is part and partial a consequence of their history and is not something that can be bred out of them in a generation or two. Their outlook is based on the wide variety of failures that surround them: Governments have always failed the people. The west is perceived to be corrupt and thus has failed their people. Japanese society is a large and wide swath that includes nearly everyone. No one is different; no one is special; no one stands out, so society, too, has failed the people. Though you are raised to trust no one, when put in a circumstance where foreigners surround you, you instinctively trust your own people and implicitly so.

Company lines are replaced by international ones.

The government makes sure to the largest extent it can that the wealth of Japan stays, for the most part, in Japan. To be sure there is a great deal of investment overseas, but by and large they are investments in real estate where the banks, in the end, hold the paper. At one point during the early 21st century, the government tried to spur spending and the flow of money by a program called the "Big Bang." It was more like a "poof." No one stirred their savings into action by investing in overseas funds or stocks or bonds.

Keep in mind that the word "risk" does not appear in the Japanese language in the sense that you and I think of it. There are words that represent "dangerous situation" or dangerous things," but these do not carry with them the implicit and explicit meaning that impacts us as native speakers when we hear the word "risk" uttered. There has been no need for a word like this to exist; the Japanese rarely take risks in the course of business.

Now while all forgoing borders on exaggeration, there is a nugget of truth in it. The fear of the "one mistake" has anyone and everyone involved in the decision-making chain fearing that the use of instinct or gut feeling as a tool will condemn them to the pool of superfluous employees in their company. It is better to do nothing and let an asset go to seed rather than risk it in a business enterprise only to have it fail in the end. While this fails the common-sense test for us and our western sensibilities—after all, in this kind of situation what do you have to lose—it makes perfect sense in a Japanese businessman's ordered world. One does not willingly expose any part of the company to public failure, even if that part is already an acknowledged failure internally. It simply isn't done. But this is what you are asking them to do when you take an asset from them and place it in a venture-backed company. The perception of value does not increase if we take a product or company and hide it under a rock. No, it happens when we laud it from every street corner, shout its praises from every mountain top, and generally broadcast it globally. Thus, we draw the attention of the financiers we need to lay down the cash in order to take the item to market.

The limit of the stake a company can traditionally own has been 20%. Furthermore, they resist have a voting board seat. An observer seat is fine. These limits allow the company to escape the obligation of having to report profits and losses as part of their own balance sheet under Japanese tax law. This creates some very difficult financing. If you are dealing with a large company, it may not pose any inconvenience. A small- to mid-sized company, on the other hand, will be a bit stressed with the paperwork. All in all, they would prefer to just limit their stake in the enterprise.

At first glance, this seems all quite neat and tidy. But the thing that will strike those with VC experience is that the value of the asset to the Japanese licensor will be proportional to the funding raised. If the VC expects a certain return on the asset, careful attention needs to be paid to the type of security issued for the actual cash invest.

The absence of a board seat may at first seem like a boon: An asset without the oversight of a bothersome voting board member. The fact that a Japanese company does not have or is reluctant to have a board member will not diminish the licensor's desire to keep some kind of control and be able to weigh in heavily on the development or the commercialization of its asset. At least in the near term. No, it would be far better to have a member of the Japanese company sit on the board than to have to devise a novel system to allow the Japanese company to retain some control over the future of its divested or licensed asset. In this respect you limit your dialogue to just one person.

Common solutions to these problems offered by the Japanese company can range from maintaining a veto power over certain decisions made by the board and the use of independent board members with at least one acting as the chairman. The challenge is to satisfy the Japanese in their quest for "control" while minimizing how many concessions on your part impacts the vital operations of the NewCo.

The Japanese are also sensitive to the idea of sublicensing. Their innate paranoia dictates that they will need to approve any sublicensing or, by extension, M&A activity that the NewCo undertakes. This seems strange for a product that the Japanese company wanted to either divest or license out, but their reasons are two-fold: (i) that their "technology" does not fall into "enemy" hands; and (ii) that an M&A activity may have the potential of marginalizing their product. The first reason is a bit absurd, but understandable while the second does make some good sense. Nobody wants their licensee to merge or acquire an entity that has any competing products. This can threaten the life cycle of the product and runs the risk of decreasing revenues.

So, they'll likely ask that you return the product if an M&A occurs, especially if it's an "M." Part of the reason why the Japanese want the product back, or least an option to take it back, is because the deal was with you, not with some other company. What do they know of this company? Nothing. They are strangers whose intentions towards the asset in question are…well…in question. Again, it's the fear of being marginalized. They want to have the same degree of attention given to the product in the new company as it was in yours. And sometimes that's just not going to be possible. There is no avoiding or assuaging the Japanese on this. Don't even try. There are, however, ways to more or less circumvent this. The difficult part as the lead investor is to sell the idea to the investor syndicate.

One solution is to limit the point during development or commercialization when they can oppose a merger or acquisition. Pick a reasonable milestone in the development or lifecycle of the product and use that as a limit. Be sure that the Japanese firm gets value at this milestone and that it is far enough along to have a better than even odds chance of success. Another, less appetizing way, is to give the Japanese company a veto power but link it to a few concrete items. Items you can readily produce regarding your future partner. The financial health of the new company, its track record in developing or selling products like yours, or its ability to integrate their product as a priority into its product portfolio. These are a few examples you can use to limit an

M&A veto. Naturally, in the definitive text you'll want to be sure to incorporate sufficiently vague text as to give you some wiggle room; e.g., "X company shall approve any M&A activity provided that such approval not to be unreasonably withheld based on the merging or acquiring company's ability to…"

Creating a venture-backed company is a work of art. No two are the same and while there is a base formula for putting a company together, it needs to be significantly modified on a case-by-case basis to such an extent that we can very plainly say that there is no play book. And this is just in the realm of our home market. When adding the Japanese variable into the equation, you have really challenged yourself.

Poaching in VC

So you managed to convince a Japanese company that your venture-backed organization is able to take one of their developmental products and successfully bring it to market in the US. Congratulations! You're already part of an elite group. Now you're wondering how the hell are you going to cope with getting all the information you need to pursue this development. Since you've gotten this far, it is reasonable to assume you understand just how difficult this will likely be. The challenge as you move forward is to: (i) have and maintain good communications; and (ii) get the information and/or materials you require in a timely manner so as to keep you on time and on target with your own goals.

One method is to have an employee of the Japanese company come and work for you. There are advantages and disadvantages to this as well as a number of ways to approach it.

Obviously, having an experienced member of the Japanese company located with you at your office facilitates the communication between your two operations. You needn't worry about miscommunications in e-mails or struggling to make yourself understood over the phone. Your Japanese employee can handle all that in his native language. It's by far easier to get your point across to a semi-competent English speaking Japanese person face-to-face than to try to convey the same message over electronic media. You can gauge each other's message through gestures and body language, tone of voice and, if necessary, the use of the ever-helpful white board with its diagrams. He, in turn, can put this into a linguistic and cultural context, and relay that to his comrades in Japan. Ideally, this would be a smooth, well oiled mechanism that would save you countless days exchanging e-mails, phone calls or whatever just to get a simple message across.

Having your own personal Japanese aide also goes a long way into avoiding making mistakes based on assumptions. By this I mean that, as westerners, we are generally flexible in approaches but tend to be intolerant of processes that are grossly disparate from our own. This may be a bit harsh. Perhaps it is better to say that we are ignorant of processes that are diametrically opposite the ones we use. Even should you have years and years experience with the Japanese culture, it does little to prepare you for really being immersed in its corporate culture. Until you actually partner with a Japanese firm, you are only seeing the tip of the iceberg. After signing an agreement, the rest suddenly hits you like you were the Titanic. But we—and people in generally—operate out of their own points of reference. So much so that it comes naturally and anything that lies a good deal outside that box seems idiotic.

But on an intellectual level we know that this isn't idiotic. Different isn't necessarily wrong, it's only different. That doesn't *preclude* it from being wrong, it only means that being wrong doesn't immediately follow. Having someone within your grasp, so to speak, who can explain the system to you and walk you through the processes—however strange and convoluted these may seem—is a great help in saving time, energy and a great many frustrating e-mails. It also goes a long way in accomplishing your mutual goals and achieving ultimate success.

There are downsides to having a native on board that bear mentioning. It is likely that you will want the Japanese individual cohabitating the office out of which you work. This means he'll need to live in your town. Having a Japanese national living in the US is like you moving to the moon. There is not much frame of reference from which the person can draw. It can be a catastrophe. Most Japanese are not very good at driving, especially the men who rely more on public transportation or their wives to get them from point A to point B. And under adverse road conditions—and to them that may mean simply moving at 65 or 70 mph as Japanese road speeds tend to be much lower than the west—the Japanese, in general, are not very good at accomplishing this task without some sort of mishap. Conditions found in the northern parts of the US will seem like Perry's expedition to the North Pole compared to the mild conditions found in the majority of the Japanese archipelago.

There are a great many other things that we, as

westerners, take for granted but that are absolutely foreign ideas to the Japanese. Alcohol etiquette is much different, so much so that it is not uncommon for a Japanese ex-patriate to get into a bit of trouble with the local law enforcement types for public drunkenness or open container, both of which are completely acceptable in Japan. Public urination, common throughout Japan, can land your new employee in the trouble, especially if it is alcohol related. Personal hygiene, the treatment of women, smoking incessantly, and the carrying around of copious amounts of cash are just a few more examples of habits that can be issues.

Aside from the everyday "dangers" of the west that we tend to tolerate and oftentimes ignore, there is always the ubiquitous language problem. Yes, you've employed this person because of his ability to serve as a linguistic and/or technical bridge between you and the Japanese licensor, but it bears keeping in mind that much of the person's English ability will be centered around the area of industry in which he is engaged. A scientist in biotechnology will be great at getting you all kinds of chemistry, manufacturing, and control information, but I doubt he could muster enough vocabulary or grammar to negotiate a call with the utility company.

As we have discussed earlier, the meaning behind the spoken words is a far, far different thing between Japanese and English. We tend to mean what we say. It is laced, more often than not, with idioms and is dripping with sarcasm, but it doesn't require a great deal of thought to understand just exactly what we are trying to convey. The Japanese, on the other hand, will take what you say to the *nth* degree and arrive at a wholly different conclusion as to what you really mean. Not what you said, but to what you are really alluding. From this errant thinking process, a host of miscommunications will result. Best to keep the language simple, brief and "standard"; that is, no expression like "cat got your tongue" or the like.

Now, if you decide that the pros outweigh the cons, and you are ready to take a Japanese on board, there are a few ways you can so this. You can source a third-party employee, that is, someone not already associated with the company with which you are doing the transaction, or you can get someone from the company who is familiar with the history of the deal and knows something about the product you are getting. Naturally the latter is the better albeit the riskier. And I say "risky" for a few reasons: (i) it depends how you hire this person; (ii) it depends on how this person is perceived at the Japanese company; and (iii) it depends how much control you have over the product in your licensed/acquired territory.

Many companies prefer to take on the Japanese employee as one of their own. This requires the Japanese person to leave his present employment and move lock, stock, and barrel to the new entity. This is all well and good if your organization is quite large and well-established in your particular industry; however, from a certain Japanese point of view this is not appealing—no matter what the potential payout is. The point of view of which I speak is not that of the salaryman, but of his wife. Typically, most going concerns in Japan still subscribe to the life-long employment system despite what you may hear of changing trends. Yes, some are looking for ways to cull positions, but it rarely comes in the form of out-and-out firings. Generally, this is accomplished to a degree of satisfaction through early retirements and attrition. With this life-long employment comes your pension. Retirement in Japan means more than just collecting a pension. Upon retirement, the majority of Japanese employees receive something called a "*taishokukin*." This is a lump sum payment that is a "thank you" for a lifetime commitment to the company. The payment can add up to quite a tidy sum. If an employee prematurely and of his own accord leaves the company, this money may be forfeit. If an employee leaves the company to work for a competitor or work for an affiliate (without permission), he will almost certainly lose this money.

Another hurdle to hiring is the housewife. Most employees you would be interested in hiring will be middle-aged and likely will have a number of monthly expenses that are inescapable, such as higher education payments for his children and a mortgage. The idea that he will leave a position that amply provides for these needs in order to move to a position that has a stability factor of about two to four years with the potential—but not guarantee—of a large cash payment at the end does not appeal to Japanese housewives on whose shoulders the burden of household expenses fall. They are not willing to take the risks part and parcel because this kind of gambit is virtually unheard of in Japan, and the precedence for doing this comes more in the way of cautionary tales whose morals include disaster and failure and not success and prosperity.

From my observations, what will happen in your efforts to lure a Japanese worker to your start-up goes something like this: The Japanese employee you approach will be enthusiastic. Consider this his mid-life crisis. He is thrilled to be bucking the system and dare all to be a part of such a venture. It is likely that he will even start negotiations with you and go so far as to be on the verge of signing a contract. Suddenly, you'll get a call informing you that he cannot take the position. He may or may not explain the reasons why, but you can be sure that it is due a great deal to one or both of two factors: (i) spousal influence; and (ii) corporate/peer pressure.

In the midst of this there is a potential to sour the deal, particularly if you are poaching while the deal is yet unsigned. You more than risk being discovered. Almost certainly you will be found out. This will be met with severe consequences in Japan. As a matter of course, loyalties in Japan go unquestioned. That an employee would entertain a move is a *de facto* betrayal. He may lose his job or, more than likely, be taken off the project and assigned to some corner somewhere in the company where he can watch paint peel for the remainder of his time. The deal itself may come to a screeching halt. If not, certainly trust, faith, and confidence will have been caustically eroded. As we have already mentioned, these intangible components are vital to doing business in Japan.

The best approach to this, if feasible by the Japanese company, is to get someone "attached" to you. In Japanese, this is called *"shukkou."* The employee is still retained by the parent Japanese company, but you pay his expenses. Additionally, his loyalties, to the extent possible, are also transferred to you. You can now rely on his full commitment to the project just so long as what you ask of him does not endanger his retirement bonus or risk alienation from the parent company. When you are done with him, you simply return him to the home company. Neat. Clean. Simple. And it doesn't put the deal at risk.

The problem with this is how the salaryman assigned to you is perceived by the Japanese company. You don't want the untouchables, which they are apt to send you. You want someone functional and someone who is taken seriously by his former colleagues. Unfortunately, like any other organization, they do not want to give away the best in talent. Many companies would look at this as an opportunity to pawn off someone they have deemed as less than useful, but who has attained a high enough position to make him seem credible. This person will be a lot of show but not much in the way of productivity. Years of being cast aside in the Japanese company will have compounded this problem. He may not be well connected to the units with which you need to interface, and he may be a bit philosophic; that is, heavy on theory and light on the application.

No matter who you get or how you get your Japanese employee, somewhere in the back of your mind never forget where his true loyalties lie: With his retirement bonus.

Alliance Management

The Japanese sense of alliance management is still a work in progress. They really don't have a grasp of the fundamental ideas behind what makes a successful partnership. I am now, of course, speaking of the small- to mid-level companies. The larger concerns have, by trial and error, developed a kind of feeling for what the "foreigners" want/expect. This may not be in tune with what the Japanese have in mind, but it is tolerated all the same, largely due to the revenue that can be had by foreign business as compared to the chokingly restrictive domestic Japanese market.

As a matter of course, most western companies have an alliance management system in place. It always helps to ensure the success of the enterprise as well as a continued well-being among the participating parties. As this has been the case for quite a number of years now, the western concept of alliance management has evolved into something of a science. Less "using the force" and more relying on tried-and-true formulae. The problem you will often encounter in prescribing an alliance management system to a modern-day Japanese company that it may seem like a bit of magic. Many ideas will be met with resistance ranging from "no one person can do what you are proposing" to re-tooling the proposal to fit the consensus oriented Japanese social and business psyche.

So how to do this. It is an educational process that will be, by definition, laced with failure. Patience and persistence will win the day. This attitude, while correct and healthy can be inadvertently spackled with an attitude of patronization. Always be on guard against this attitude and never, ever think yourself above it. All things start with good intentions. You will be infected to some extent. Be assured of that. When you catch yourself developing this kind of perspective, back off and take a well-deserved breather. Remember. Japan is a country of facades. It is difficult to tell what is going on under the surface. Remember the concepts of the *tatamae* and the *honne*.

As with all things foreign, the Japanese work well if the system is laid out in writing. It is something for them to study and something for them to hold up in argument. I'm not sure an SOP would be appropriate, although from a Japanese perspective SOPs are always preferable. On the downside, it will be something that the Japanese will treat like the Word of God; that is, never allowing for unique circumstances to deviate from the written word. You will not have much leeway if you decide later to stray from this original text even if it is in the best interest of the project. It will take an amendment and no small amount of time to get that done.

In whatever way you finally decide to manage the project, keep in the back of your mind that the Japanese are not very flexible and do not react quickly to fluid situations. Factor that into whatever strategy you adopt to remain in control of the asset and the collaboration. With a bit of forethought and with some thorough prior planning, this rigidity can be overcome—and sometimes used to an advantage. To best do this, you will need to identify what is the most important aspect of the deal from your Japanese partner's perspective and key in on that. It may not be all that obvious. We, in the west, tend to think in terms of bottom line and that all too often translates in profits. In a country that is perpetually financed by the banking institutions, cash is not such a problem. Companies today can still operate in the red for a number of years despite the so-called banking reforms of the recent past. From a Japanese perspective, the selection of one company over another as a partner is not necessarily a matter of better financials. This does play an integral role, but the real value comes in how a particular candidate can add value to the Japanese company's home market position. Small- to mid-sized Japanese companies are still at a point where the domestic market is their main focus. Yes, they may have visions of dancing on the global stage, but they are not about to do that without first establishing themselves nationally. Earning the respect of their peers at home is worth more to a mainstream Japanese company than all the billions that could be made abroad. Reputation and prestige carry more weight in Japan than cash.

That is not to say that they won't be in your face every minute wanting to know where their royalty payments are. Money is important. Be prepared for rigid and unforgiving payment schedules. Brace yourself against the horde of e-mails and phone calls checking up on the smallest of progress. Hedge yourself against the innumerable meetings that your counterparts will want to hold throughout the year.

This last point deserves comment.

The Japanese, being a consensus driven society in virtually every regard, will want to convene several meetings throughout the year to discuss the project and offer suggestions on how you can better succeed in a market with which they are completely unfamiliar. Whether you are in the US or the EU, these meetings will eat into your schedules like a cancer. Assuming you are the one traveling, and if you consider travel time, a one-day meeting turns into a four-day affair. Naturally, most of us do not object to meeting when the agenda is full enough to warrant one, but I think I am fairly safe in assuming that no one wants to spend ten grand and four days for a four-hour conversation and an expensive dinner.

To avoid having to deal with these requests for meetings *ad nauseam*, draft something sane in the agreement. I doubt that the Japanese will put up much of a fight during the negotiation for the meeting frequencies. If they are experienced enough with deals, they'll appreciate that the meetings are well spaced apart throughout a year. The urgency for meetings only arises after the contract is signed. It's at this time that the stress of having to conclude a deal starts to bleed off and they realize that there is nothing to do. They'll have powered down and will feel obligated to do something. This will predicate meetings. You can also expect a slew of e-mails or faxes.

Probably as with any successful alliance management, choosing the right manager is key. You want someone that is, above all, patient, charismatic, nonconfrontational, and respectful. A Japanese alliance will take a greater portion of his or her time than other partnerships and alliances, so be sure not to give it to someone who has demonstrated the bandwidth needed.

Work the agreement so that your obligation to communicate your ongoing activities is at a minimum. Choose a corresponding medium that is convenient. Make it easy for your Japanese partners to use that medium. If you choose to use telephone teleconferences, make sure the sound quality is good and use a conferencing service to allow several sites in Japan to dial in rather than force them all to come together. Choose times that are convenient for the Japanese rather than for yourself. If you use a video teleconferencing facility, make sure that you can work so the participants attending from your side have clear transmissions of their faces. The idea is to put your Japanese partners at ease and to clearly and succinctly transmit the information one time, with no need to have a mountain of e-mails ensue because no one really understood what happened at the conference.

No matter what venue you choose for your meetings, there are three basic tenets to having clear communication with the Japanese: (i) summarize; (ii) summarize; and (iii) summarize.

As best you can, summarize the material brought to the table for discussion. Try to give top line information only and save the detailed stuff for written communiqués. This prevents the meeting from being too long. A drawn-out discussion in a foreign language wears down your attention span quickly and all that you will be left with after about an hour are nodding heads.

Summarize as you go to close out one topic before entering another. This prevents all the items from being blurred together and eventually leading to having either you or your Japanese counterparts being lost. Once lost, it is virtually impossible to recover.

Summarize the key points and action items at the end of the meeting. As when we were looking at meetings during the negotiation part of the deal, never, let them do the summarizing. Make sure you take copious notes throughout and very briefly run through the items covered, decisions made, and actions items agreed upon. This last item includes who is to perform the task and by when.

Of course, each meeting is different and there will be times when they will need to be long. This is inevitable. For those, face-to-face meetings are probably best and those are best strung out over a couple/few days. In these instances, travel is unavoidable but well worth it to avoid the strain of having to do the same task again but over a much longer period of time and through massive volumes of clarifying correspondences.

Alliance management will, in some way, shape, or form, need to be implemented in any deal you conclude with the Japanese. You're going to want this for a plethora of reasons but the foremost is to create some kind of buffer—or, more accurately, a filter—to keep at bay the avalanche of requests, clarifications, proposals, and amendments coming from their side. You need to have some space to do your thing, and your thing is to either develop a product, commercialize it, or further partner it. This leads to success for both you and your Japanese partner no matter what their focus is. Putting a firewall up in the form of alliance management will help you do this. Your manager can discern want really needs immediate attention and what can wait a half-year.

Of the two parties, you are the creative one. Use this to devise an alliance management scheme that works and that is flexible. Your new partner will hound you at every turn if you give them the chance. Build in buffers and periodic reporting time points to take this daily pressure off. The last thing you want after doing a deal with a Japanese company is to develop a dread of opening e-mails. Well defined and detailed procedures laid out in the definitive agreement is the key. It must clear, comprehensible, and simple enough for a child to follow. Only in this fashion can you preempt the nagging and constant inquiries into the mundane, day-to-day detail of the project.

The Future

Nobody knows the future. This is a phrase often used by the Japanese, and you would expect nothing less from a culture that fostered Zen Buddhism. A business example of this is when you want them to explain some of their market research. You look at their results and see that they encompass a very, very broad range. So broad as to make the data unusable. When questioned as to why their assumptions in this research were so nebulous, the reply will inevitably be, "Nobody knows the future."

And that's true. But it is just because we can't divine future events that we do the research in the first place. While we can't see clearly what will happen, we can make a number of predictions that are close enough to actual events so as to make the future manageable. Every one of us, I believe, harbors no delusions that we actually control anything outside our sphere of influence. Even within that realm, sometimes the best we can do is prod events in a certain direction. Because of this lack of omnipotence, we develop mechanisms to manage and reduce the risks involved with the unknown to the greatest extent possible. Some of these mechanisms are tried and true, while some are as individual as the person using them. Some are based on science and generations of research while others are mystical and border on voodoo. But whatever the case, it is human nature to endeavor to form and shape events to our benefit.

The Japanese have a hard time grasping these concepts much less committing to them. Anything that is not obvious, in the western sense of obviousness, will almost certainly be lost on the Japanese. Despite the neat gadgets and toys that this manufacturing society pumps out, they are by their very nature, a people engrossed in routines and consistency. Improving and adapting are qualities possessed by the Japanese that are universally acknowledged; however, these qualities do not extend into society itself. This is another example of the dichotomy of the people. The social strata, as we have already discussed, has not progressed much since the 16th century. The costumes and environs have changed, but the overall operation of the culture has not. This gives them a certain resiliency in their thought patterns. Some authors have even gone so far as to say that it is something genetic. While a bit outlandish, there is some credence that the maintaining of such a homologous culture has removed the agility of the Japanese to adjust their perspective. It is difficult for them to look at a situation from different angles. It's not that they are obtuse or that they refuse, but that they simply don't know how. It goes back to the axiom, "You don't know what you don't know."

There is an advantage in living in a world where

borders are drawn by politics and not by cultures. We find a number of different cultures living side-by-side in a kind of harmony. There is a much greater give and take. There has to be. But when dealing with the Japanese, it is worth bearing in mind that we westerners did not develop this kind of social tolerance *via* a superior nature. This ability came at the expense of millions of lives lost in countless violent confrontations with our neighbors. We are a people born out of war. To some extent, the Japanese are as well, but whereas they fought internally for control of their island nation, we fought for ideals, largely political and religious ones. We've had our fair share of land disputes, but for us it was about overwriting our ethos on our neighbors. To be the prevailing culture. The Japanese had only one culture to begin with making that kind of contest a bit moot. These two warpaths lead in different directions. Westerners have had to come to grips with the fact that there are going to be people in the world who believe in different things and express themselves in different ways. And sometimes, these people may live next door. For the Japanese living before 1858, these kinds of different people were something out of the fairy tale books.

If there is a problem with a contract, or with the conditions of a deal, it needs to be something that you can present to your Japanese partner without having to follow an extensive line of reasoning. Following that kind of threaded argument is rarely within the ability of an average Japanese professional. And what do I mean by that? Let me give a real-life example. I was working in the licensing department of a Japanese company and I was analyzing an agreement that had been negotiated and executed without

210

my assistance. This involved a US-venture company and centered around a product for which there are a number of different uses. Looking at the sales milestones and looking at the total market revenue for the applications for which the product was being used, and comparing that to the market share the company presently held, the numbers simply did not add up. There were a number of sales milestones that would never be reached. The US company was sage enough to put these in there as "teasers" and the Japanese staff negotiating the deal had no idea they were fictional points. Sure, they looked good in the context of the agreement and they seemed to add to the overall deal value—rather potential deal value, but were just not in the realm of achievement. Furthermore, there was uncertainty in the way the licensed product was to be used in combination with a product the company already had on the market. Since these were both high-end items and were subject to reimbursements, it was unlikely that any reimbursement organization would shell out twice the cost for less than twice the improvement. In other words, the added value of the second product did not equate to a two-fold increase in the performance of the first. Therefore, the product we licensed would only be used to enhance the first. To do this, the quantity of our product needed to do this would be relatively minute.

The US company knew that. They structured the royalty arrangement so that using the product alone—something that seemed dubious in light of them just beginning the marketing of their first and similar product—would garner us an above average royalty rate for the industry. Even a bit attractive. On the other hand, if it were used in conjunction with another product, it would earn a *pro rata* royalty based on the compound's contribution to the value of the combination product. So theoretically, if the original royalty was 15% and the product was sold for $100 by itself, then you would receive $15. But in this scheme, if the product were used in conjunction with another product and increased the value of the other product by 10%—from $100 to $110—the royalty receive is 15% of $10, or $1.50.

Seems fairly straightforward, doesn't it? But it's not necessarily a meat-and-potatoes deal; that is, something that is run of the mill. It was unique and a little convoluted. Part of the problem was the context in which the original conditions were framed; they were sufficiently complex that the Japanese BDL group had difficulty understanding them and, by extension, translating them for their senior management. The second problem is that a number of hypothetical events needed to be analyzed which would've led to the realization that the deal was flawed. The third and most difficult problem is to look at the deal from a different perspective; that is; in context of the market and the marketplace. It requires that you have an idea of how things work in a different cultural setting and drawing conclusions from this. Unless the hole in the agreement is big enough to drive a Mac Truck through, the Japanese may not to see it without help.

But let's talk about your future for a minute. I mean, the reason you've decided to engage a Japanese company in a business transaction is, I would assume, primarily because you are looking to broaden your horizons and increase your potential as a company as you move forward into the future. The difference between success and failure is being able to walk into the deal with your eyes wide open. Business development is sometimes characterized as managing expectations. Whether you are in charge or you are a proxy, your key to a win-win situation is managing what each party expects from the deal and ensuring that those expectations are satisfied, in one form or another. That is easier said than done. From your side, the expectations have probably been laid out to you clear as crystal. They may change and adapt to the circumstances encountered as you collectively move down the road from imagination to reality, but most western BDL guys have a pretty high confidence level of what is expected of them and what the company, in turn, is expecting. Unfortunately, the same cannot be said of your Japanese counterparts. Even their BDL staff may not know the entire strategy and, consequently, will not be able to communicate that to you. Like a good drama, this will unfold as the deal progresses. Your job will be to look through the mist and give form and shape to their expectations at the earliest possible time. This will allow you to successfully lift and shift your negotiating strategy as well as find creative ways to give both parties what they want.

There are some key indicators that help in this situation. First, look at the monetary recompense last. It is rare that a mid-level company will enter a deal with a foreign company just on the basis of money. There are a great number of reasons why money is likely not the center piece. Among the possible reasons for doing a deal with a western company are (i) gaining access to data that is more cheaply obtained overseas than in Japan; (ii) for a *quid pro quo* product; (iii) to increase its international profile; (iv) to shore up its worth in the face of possible mergers; or (v) to divest a product that it would otherwise have to scrap. Money, in these scenarios, is a secondary issue. But make no mistake. While money may be a secondary issue or even an afterthought, when the time comes to negotiate the terms for the value, you can be certain that they will put up a formidable fight to get as much as they can.

So, when it comes to discussing events and financials of the future, let the Japanese ponder the unknown ramifications. You, meanwhile, build scenarios and use every business tool at your disposal to manage the variables that lie in that future. Planning, familiarity with the markets, and an honest assessment of your own capabilities all help, but they only get you part of the way there; especially, when you are interacting with or relying on the cooperation of a Japanese firm. Add to these a firm grasp of who your partner is, what he is able to contribute, to what lengths he is willing to go to ensure success, and what is his end game, and you should find yourself on the brink of success.

A Few Last Words

If you find the need to move into the Japanese market to locate products to sell in your market, brace yourself. Get, as much as possible beforehand, a good feel for the country, customs, and business practices. This is a large task in and of itself since all the elements are dramatically different than the ones with which you are so familiar. Book learning—and that, unfortunately includes this one—can only get you so far. It's like an infantry lieutenant doing a map reconnaissance. The diagram can tell you only so much; the details come only with the familiarity of boots on ground. How does this apply to your situation? Well, the task is very much the same: You are trying to get the lay of the land, a feel for what kind of obstacles may lie between you and your final goal; where things may lie in ambush; where there are blind spots; black zones for your communications; and safe havens for rally points.

All this can be accomplished by your first swing through Japan when you either are giving the initial pitch for your product or are looking for that one particular opportunity that best fits your corporate needs. This first trip to Japan is a freebie. You are expected and entitled to be a greenhorn. Make as many mistakes as you can this trip. I'm not saying that these should be deliberate, but they should be tactical. Even the best preparation is no substitute for actual experience. You will have, undoubtedly, identified tasks both socially and in business that will require repeated execution; for example, the exchange of business cards, the sitting at tables, the knowledge of when something (like a meeting) is finished and then the summarization and conclusion of a function (like a meeting or a dinner). Too many people try to fit in from the very beginning without first trying to get a sense of how far they can push something or before they get a good feel of the range of acceptable behavior for a particular circumstance. Instead, they try to achieve the ideal of the situation. This rigid interpretation will lead to a number of *faux pas* well past the time the Japanese are expecting you to master these, sometimes, very simple tasks.

I hope that your first outing is not only successful but relatively trouble free. I don't mean to insinuate that everything goes as smooth as silk, but rather that everything falls into the "expected and manageable" category. If it does not go well, be of good cheer; it could be a function of the company you are dealing with. Things will also get better the next time around. Dress rehearsals are best, if time is a luxury you have. Before doing the $500 million deal, do the $30 million deal. If you flub the latter, the lessons learned will make the chances of succeeding at the former much higher. Moreover, while

$30 million is not chump change, its loss pales in comparison to $500 million.

Whatever you do and whatever your reason for doing it, do not approach this type of deal-making with an aloof, by the numbers attitude. If you aren't careful, these deals can take literally years to finish. Most of us do not have that kind of time or patience. And don't think that just because you've been victorious on three continents that Asia—Japan in particular—will be just another venue ripe for your corporate carpet-bombing. There is a reason why we still refer to this region as the Far East, even in today's supersonic jet age. It's as close as some of us will ever get at visiting another planet.

I hope that some of these insights were useful and you can use them to your advantage as you grope your way through the darkness we call Japan Inc. No single work can fully prep you for what you will encounter. If it could, I doubt anyone could master it in the time you have on Earth. But having a basic understanding can lay the foundation for the experience and information you amass during your interaction with the country and the people of Japan.

A word of warning from someone who has lived too long amongst these people: Japan is a here and now opportunity. The country is on a collision course with itself unless it manages some internal change. They've leverage everything out of their financial institutions. There is a recent shift in population distribution resulting in an inverse pyramid structure. With the longevity of the people being one of the highest in the world—at least for the present elderly generation—and with their socialist system, the upcoming generation will need to fund retirements and health plans not only for themselves but for the preceding generations. Japan is still a manufacturing centric economy in a world of soft products and intellectual property. The future lies in the exploitation of bits, bytes, electrons and photons, not in cars. The country is running up the largest deficit in the world. Someday the payment is going to be due. As the end draws near, I predict that the environment will become even more hostile to western corporate influences. They will blame the rest of the world for raping them. There will be no saviors emerging from Japan and they will instinctively shun the western messiahs. Despite a hopeless situation, the pride of the Japanese would have them prefer to get bounced back to the Stone Age before they let foreign influence take over their economic system.

For the time being, Japan can be a source of good opportunities for both for buying and selling. Me? I recommend buying for your own market. In this way you are not slave to the Japanese economic system. It's only a matter of finding the right match and understanding the differences between expectations. Make no assumptions and be careful to screen carefully your own thought process to weed out the reflexive western ideologies. In six months, you are not going to overwrite your western philosophies on a people that have adhered to the same basic credo for 1500 years.

Finally, I'd like to begin as I started: By saying this is not meant to be a critical of Japan and its culture. It is only meant to let western business types understand what they are walking into when they consider a collaboration with a Japanese company. I think that you will find that you can accomplish a great deal with this in mind. It also helps to display a certain amount of mutual respect and, if you can muster it, admiration along the way. In no other culture is this so essential as in the Japanese culture. No matter how much you may grow annoyed with their mannerisms, no matter how much you may come to disdain their circular logic, no matter how incongruous the arguments, no matter how superior their attitudes, and no matter how layered the truth appears, if you walk in the foreknowledge of all this and understand that all of these are neither consciously nor maliciously done but is a virtue of their culture, you will certainly not only succeed in your undertaking, but will have perhaps a most loyal and diligent partner. Sir Francis Bacon once said, "Knowledge is power." In no other business arena can this axiom be shown true than in the coliseum where modern-day gladiators duke it out for Japanese business. Empower yourself before entering this fray. Get to know a bit about the culture and the company first hand, because even though you can read about it, first hand intelligence is the best and most useful kind. So, gird yourself, prepare yourself, and go get yourself some business.

About the Author

Mark Smith originally found work in Japan as a teacher for a private English conversation school in Fuji, Japan. He was soon was offered a job in the business development and licensing group of the pharmaceutical division of a blue-chip Japanese corporation. This began a career that would span 15 years. Beginning as a cultural and English language resource interacting with western companies, Mark spent years as a business development project manager. After being an integral part of a venture capital spinout, he served as a board observer and later a managing director for the new company. During that time, he also worked in the New York corporate office as a Vice President of Business Development. Upon negotiating the reacquisition of an asset, Mark worked as the Vice President of General Affairs, Corporate Secretary, and Vice President of Business Development of the Boston subsidiary formed to develop the asset.

In 2013, Mark formed Global Pharma Solutions, LLC (GPS) which provides a bridge for western companies trying to make forays in the Japanese market and *vice versa*.

GPS also provides operational, planning, and business development services for pharmaceutical start-ups and venture capital backed companies. In this capacity, he has served as Corporate Secretary, Chief Financial Officer, Chief Business Officer, and Director of Human Resources.

Mark is the author of *To Form a Perfect Union: The Forgotten American Social Contract.*

Made in the USA
Monee, IL
17 May 2022

96552958R00129

Mysteries of the Rosary
in Ordinary Life